The Bald Soprano
and
The Lesson

Works by Eugène Ionesco
Published by Grove Press

Exit the King, The Killer, and MacBett
(Translated by Charles Marowitz and Donald Watson)

Rhinoceros and Other Plays
(Translated by Derek Prouse and including *The Leader; The Future Is in Eggs or It Takes All Sorts to Make a World*)

Three Plays
(Translated by Donald Watson and including *Amédéé; The New Tenant; Victims of Duty*)

The Bald Soprano
and
The Lesson

EUGÈNE IONESCO

TRANSLATED FROM THE FRENCH BY TINA HOWE

Grove Press
New York

CONTENTS

Acknowledgments

Grateful acknowledgment is made to my long time producer Robyn Goodman, who first suggested I tackle these translations, to the Theatre Communications Group for funding them, to my hero, Christian Parker, for bringing them to the Atlantic Theater Company, to Neil Pepe for having the courage to produce them, to Carl Forsman for directing them, to the cast, designers, and crew for bringing them to stunning life, to Rosette Lamont and Françoise Kourilsky, my inspired French readers, to Claudia Orenstein for casting me as the Maid in a student production of *The Bald Soprano* at Hunter College, realizing my lifelong dream of being *in* an Ionesco play, to my agent, Patrick Herold for finessing this publication, to Grove/Atlantic for embracing it, and finally, to my husband, Norman, for bearing with me midst this delirium.

INTRODUCTION

On the eve of Ionesco's triumphant 1960 London opening of *Rhinoceros,* directed by Orson Welles and starring Laurence Olivier, the eminent critic Martin Esslin approached Madame Ionesco and remarked on how happy her husband must be.

"On the contrary," she replied. "He is sad."

"But why would he be sad?" Esslin asked.

"Because he's afraid of death."

This terror pierced the great Rumanian playwright Eugène Ionesco as a child and never left him. When he heard church bells peal, he thought of funerals. When he watched a hilarious Punch and Judy show, he grieved for its inevitable end. Everyone he loved was doomed to die, including himself. The burden of this morbidity was enormous and especially cruel for an artist, because the artist is supposed to explain the meaning in it all. But if he's chattering under his bed in a terror, how can he proceed? And what's the point?

Samuel Beckett was racked with similar existential despair. Both had endured the horrors of the Second World War and both were desperate to bear witness. But how? Beckett found consolation in paring things down to their essence. Ionesco's approach was the polar opposite. He went for overabundance—furniture that proliferated, corpses that kept growing and herds of rhinoceri plunging across the stage. *Herds!*

"There's something free and unfettered about excess," Ionesco wrote. "You're not eating to live, you're eating to burst."

It's this bursting that makes his work so extraordinary. The first of his plays that I saw was *The Bald Soprano,* which has now been running in Paris for fifty years at the tiny Théâtre de la Huchette. But it wasn't the characters or inanimate objects that detonated, it was language itself! The words the actors spoke kept exploding. It was like watching popping balloons—the *bang,* the sweet scent of helium and bits of rubber flying through the air— I'd never seen anything like it on stage!

The year was 1960. I'd just graduated from college and was living in Paris for the winter. Having gone to experimental schools for most of my life, I knew nothing about the theater and even less about Ionesco. And suddenly here I was, in the midst of all this delirium. What was most astonishing, however, was how deadpan the actors were. They didn't bat an eye, but soldiered on, picking their way through the rubble as if it were the most natural thing in the world. I suddenly realized why it was so funny. Because it was just like being at home!

Language tended to fly out of control in our household as well. My father, Quincy Howe, was a radio commentator on CBS in the 1940s, so on weeknights my mother and I would listen to him deliver the evening news. Wearing one of her outlandish hats and drinking a cocktail, she'd keep sighing, "Poor Daddy." I never understood her wistful response, since millions of people looked forward to his commentary, delivered in that staccato Boston accent. She was clearly in another world, but then so was I, bent over my coloring books, or melting crayons on the radiator. The disconnect between us was huge, but it never stopped us from talking.

We reveled in words! My father not only recited poetry at the drop of a hat, he taught his parakeets to spout verse as well. When I was recovering from hepatitis after my stay in Paris, he came to the hospital every day to read James Joyce's *Ulysses* aloud. He also took me to e. e. cummings poetry readings. But he had his antic side as well, since these high-minded forays were sandwiched between jaunts to Marx Brothers movies and vaudeville acts at the Palace where we'd laugh ourselves liquid watching the roller-skating midgets.

So you can imagine my delight at being plunged into a drawing room so similar to mine, but with everyone speaking French! Like my parents, the Smiths and Martins had impeccable manners, but the nonsense that came out of their mouths . . . I started laughing and soon realized the entire audience was laughing with me. Helplessly! Hysterically! Continuously! Needless to say, it was the theatrical experience of my life. I became an Ionesco disciple on the spot and had the added thrill of introducing him at the 92nd Street Y in 1986 when he did a reading of his novel *Rhinoceros*.

How then did such a depressed man come to write *The Bald Soprano*?

It all began when he was struggling to learn English from a French-English conversation manual. As he copied out the phrases the two couples were exchanging, he discovered he was learning surprising truths as well—that the ceiling is above the floor and there are seven days in the week. But then something strange started to happen:

> ". . . before my very eyes the text underwent a subtle transformation, against my will. After a time, those inspired yet simple sentences which I had so painstakingly copied into my schoolboy's exercise book, detached themselves from the pages on which they had been written, changed places all by themselves, become garbled and corrupted. . . . the lines of dialogue in the manual had got out of hand. . . . Unfortunately the wise and elementary truths they exchanged, when strung together, had gone mad, the language had become disjointed, the characters distorted; words, now absurd, had been emptied of their content. . . .

"For me, what had happened was a kind of collapse of reality. The words had turned into sounding shells devoid of meaning, the characters too of course, had been emptied of psychology and the world appeared to me in an unearthly, perhaps its true light, beyond understanding and governed by arbitrary laws.

"While writing this play (for it had become a kind of play or anti-play, that is to say a real parody of a play, a comedy of comedies), I had felt genuinely uneasy, sick and dizzy. . . . I imagined I had written something like the *tragedy of language*."★

So you can understand Ionesco's surprise when the first reading of his tragedy was greeted with laughter. This anti-play that had made him so sick was actually a *comedy*. The language was skewered, but what made it side-splitting was the characters' desperation to communicate while maintaining a stiff upper lip. No matter how much nonsense came out of their mouths, they were determined to keep up appearances. The fun begins with Mrs. Smith struggling to tell her husband about her uneventful day as he reads the newspaper. Then we're introduced to Mr. and Mrs. Martin, who can't remember if they've ever met. The miracle of these scenes—of *every* scene in the play—is that the speaker doesn't give up! Their words may be banal, repetitious or overblown, but they soldier on. And on! And *on*! If nothing's left but fractured vowels and consonants, so be it. They'll utter them with the same brio as if they were reciting Shakespeare. It's their valor that's so moving and hilarious! Like my father teaching his parakeets Gray's "Elegy Written in a Country Courtyard," which they did to perfection—with his Boston accent to boot!

★*Notes and Counter Notes: Writings on the Theatre,* by Eugène Ionesco, translated by Donald Watson, Grove Press, 1964, p. 179

When I was offered a TCG fellowship to translate *The Bald Soprano* along with *The Lesson,* it was a dream come true! If I did my job well, perhaps I could re-create the euphoria I'd experienced at the Théâtre de la Huchette. It was a daunting challenge. French is so much funnier than English because it's so chewy and spoken so fast. There's something about all those rolling r's—like speaking with a mouth full of caramel corn. When I took a group of Columbia playwriting students to a bilingual production of the play, they much preferred it in French, even though they didn't understand a word.

What makes the translator's job even trickier is maintaining the formality of these insane proceedings. Once Ionesco realized he was writing an anti-play, he saw it as an opportunity to turn boulevard theater on its head. Hence, the English drawing room and impeccable manners of everyone on stage. But how does a translator strike a balance between verbal mayhem and social formality? To say nothing about maintaining the gloss of the classic passages like the Bobby Watson riff, the Martins' attempt to figure out if they've ever met before or the Fire Captain's endless story about the head cold? You can't relax the elegance of these constructs since they're being spoken by upright Englishmen.

Take the Martins' compulsive repetition of "*Comme c'est curieux, comme c'est bizarre! Et quelle coincidence!*" To replace these exclamations with colloquialisms like "Get outta here!" "Far out!" or "You're pulling my leg!" would be sacrilege. Their amnesia is hysterical, but what makes it so funny is their sangfroid as their situation becomes more preposterous.

So, translate Ionesco literally, you say. But if one goes down that road, then all the punning, wordplay and rhyming go out the window. And why on earth would proper Englishmen indulge in French wordplay? When the Smiths and Martins start hurling gibberish at each other at the end of the play, there was no alternative but to toss out the French altogether and come up with British equivalents. Thus, Mrs. Martin's "Bazar, Balzac, Bazaine!" became "Byron, Browning, Beowulf!" For these moments, my duty was clear. I had to *become* Ionesco! I was beside myself! I suddenly had license to crawl out of my pasty New England skin and transform into a red-blooded Rumanian!

It's one thing to *read* Ionesco, picturing his characters in your mind's eye, but try *playing* them, that's when things get tricky! Since I'm a playwright myself, I stage them in my head. They leap into three, if not twenty-seven dimensions. Since the Atlantic Theater Company in New York produced these translations under the direction of Carl Forsman in 2004, I was not only translator, but dramaturge, resident psychiatrist and keeper of Ionesco's flame as well.

Performing *The Bald Soprano* is an enormous challenge for actors, particularly American actors, who are so focused on psychological truth—being in the moment. But if their dialogue breaks down and their moments lose all meaning, how do they proceed? They can't *play* absurdity. The audience will be mystified, or even worse, bored—which seems to happen more often than not when the play is staged. Amateur productions tend to disintegrate into orgies of self-indulgence, with crazy costumes and acrobatics. But Ionesco wasn't writing about the absurdity of life. He was writing about the heroism it takes to get through it.

If striking a balance between formality and dizziness in *The Bald Soprano* was difficult, maintaining a light touch in *The Lesson* was almost impossible. Once again language reigns supreme, but this time with horrifying results. In his effort to teach the Student philology, the Professor's words multiply, transmogrify and whirl completely out of control. He ends up raving like a madman. His poor student can't keep up. She literally gets sick, developing a toothache, but the more she weakens, the more florid he becomes. In a fit of frustration, he finally grabs an invisible dagger and slaughters her, ripping her body from bottom to top in a kind of ghastly rape.

In his character description, Ionesco describes the Professor as a little old man with a pointed white beard, in his fifties or sixties. He wears a pince-nez, a black skullcap, a long black schoolmaster's gown, black trousers and shoes, a detachable white collar and black tie. Since this paints such an archaic portrait, we cast a much younger actor in the Atlantic production. We kept the black graduation-type gown, but otherwise he looked like he'd just stepped out of a college classroom. The eighteen-year-old student, who's supposed to wear a gray apron and blouse with a small white collar, became a robust coed who carried a book bag instead of a briefcase. The formal tone of their exchanges remained the same, but watching this dance of death performed by actors who looked like us gave the play an added chill. So much so that as the Student writhed in pain, the more fainthearted ladies in the audience invariably fled the theater with their hands over their eyes and ears.

The Bald Soprano ends in a free-for-all of nonsense, but life goes on. The Martins return and start the play all over again reciting the Smiths' lines. In *The Lesson,* however, the language turns deadly. The word for dagger actually *becomes* the dagger that rapes and kills. But does Ionesco want us to think this assault is real? The Student is his fortieth victim that day, which is physically impossible. What makes the play so disturbing, then, isn't what happens, but the *way* it happens. Simple words put in the wrong mouths can do monstrous things.

If *The Bald Soprano* was a tragedy of language, *The Lesson* is a horror show, defying category. There's no valor here, only bloodletting and thirty-nine more caskets to fill. What an act of theatrical daring! To create characters who are at the mercy of language! Gone are the familiar Aristotelian notions of tragedy and free will.

Yet how moving and familiar these characters become! How else does one explain the gales of laughter that greet these plays after fifty years? Just try getting a seat to see them at the Théâtre de la Huchette. They're invariably sold out.

Tina Howe
November 21, 2006
New York City

THE BALD SOPRANO
AN ANTI-PLAY

The Bald Soprano premiered at the Théâtre des Noctambules on May 11, 1950 with the Compagnie Nicolas Bataille under the direction of Mr. Bataille, who also played the role of Mr. Martin.

CHARACTERS

MR. SMITH Claude Mansard

MRS. SMITH Paulette Frantz

MR. MARTIN Nicolas Bataille

MRS. MARTIN Simone Mozet

MARY, THE MAID Odette Barrois

THE FIRE CAPTAIN Henry-Jacques Huet

The translation of *The Bald Soprano* by Tina Howe had its World Premiere on September 19, 2004 at Atlantic Theater Company: Neil Pepe, Artistic Director; Andrew D. Hamingson, Managing Director; Melinda Berk, General Manager; Kurt Gardner, Production Manager; Boneau/Bryan-Brown, Press Representative. Set design was by Loy Arcenas; costume design by Theresa Squire; lighting design by Josh Bradford; sound design by Obadiah Eaves; dramaturge, Christian Parker; casting, Bernard Telsey Casting; fight director, Rick Sordelet; and production stage manager, Jennifer Grutza. Directed by Carl Forsman. The cast was as follows:

MRS. SMITH Jan Maxwell

MR. SMITH Michael Countryman

MARY, THE MAID Maggie Lacey

MR. MARTIN Robert Stanton

MRS. MARTIN Seana Kofoed

THE FIRE CAPTAIN John Ellison Conlee

Mr. and Mrs. Smith

A bourgeois drawing room in Great Britain. With British armchairs. A thoroughly British evening. MR. SMITH, British, sits in his armchair wearing his British slippers, puffing on his British pipe and reading his British newspaper next to a British fire. He sports British spectacles and a trim gray British moustache. MRS. SMITH sits beside him in another British armchair, mending some British socks. A long moment of British silence. The British clock strikes seventeen British strokes.

MRS. SMITH   Good grief, it's nine o'clock. We've eaten our soup, fish, buttered potato jackets and British salad. The children have drunk British water. We stuffed ourselves this evening. All because we live in the outskirts of London and because our name is Smith.

Mr. Smith keeps reading, clicking his tongue.

MRS. SMITH   The buttered potato jackets were delicious and the salad dressing wasn't rancid. The salad dressing they carry at the corner is higher grade than the salad dressing they carry across the street. Though I wouldn't dream of telling them it was disappointing.

Mr. Smith reads on, clicking his tongue.

MRS. SMITH   It's just the salad dressing at the corner is better.

Mr. Smith reads on, clicking his tongue.

MRS. SMITH   Mary did a lovely job with the buttered potato jackets this evening. She didn't cook them enough the last time. I prefer them crisp.

Mr. Smith reads on, clicking his tongue.

MRS. SMITH The fish was so fresh it made me drool. I had
two helpings. No, make that three. I had to run to the loo.
You also had three helpings, but you took less the third
time whereas I took much more. I ate rings around you.
What's going on? You usually eat me under the table. You
aren't lacking in the appetite department.

Mr. Smith clicks his tongue.

MRS. SMITH The soup, however, was on the salty side.
Saltier than you. Ha, ha, ha. It had too many leeks and not
enough onions. I'm sorry I didn't tell Mary to add a pinch
of anise seed. Next time I'll know better.

Mr. Smith reads on, clicking his tongue.

MRS. SMITH Our little boy was hoping for a beer. He enjoys
the buzz. Like father, like son. Did you see how he eyed
the bottle? But I filled his glass with good old British
drinking water instead. He was parched, so he drank it.
Helen takes after me: she's practical, a penny-pincher and a
piano player. She never asks for British beer. She reminds
me of our little girl who only drinks milk and only eats
porridge. Well, what do you expect? She's only two. Her
name is Peggy. The quince tart with string beans was
fantastic. We might have broken out a spot of Australian
burgundy along with it for dessert, but I don't like having
wine at the table for fear of turning the children into lushes.
They must be taught moderation and sobriety.

Mr. Smith reads on, clicking his tongue.

MRS. SMITH Mrs. Parker knows a Rumanian grocer named
Popesco Rosenfeld who just arrived from Constantinople.
He's a connoisseur of yogurt. He has a diploma from the
Andrianople Institute of Yogurt Cultures. Tomorrow I'm
going to buy a big pot of native Rumanian yogurt from

him. Opportunities like this don't pop up every day of the week, here in the outskirts of London.

Mr. Smith reads on, clicking his tongue.

MRS. SMITH   Yogurt is excellent for the stomach, the kidneys, appendicitis and apotheosis. That's what Doctor Mackenzie-King told me. He takes care of our neighbors' children, the Johns. He's a good doctor. You can trust him. He never prescribes medication he has hasn't tried on himself first. Before he operated on Parker, he operated on his own liver, even though there was nothing wrong with it.

MR. SMITH   Then how come he pulled through and Parker died?

MRS. SMITH   Because the operation was a success in his case, but not in Parker's.

MR. SMITH   Then Mackenzie-King isn't a good doctor. The operation should succeed for them both or they both should die.

MRS. SMITH   Why?

MR. SMITH   Because a conscientious doctor should die with his patients if he can't cure them. The captain of a ship goes down with his boat. Into the briny deep. He doesn't think about saving his own skin.

MRS. SMITH   You can't compare a patient with a boat!

MR. SMITH   Why not? Boats have their ailments too and your doctor is as sound as a battleship. That's why he should have gone down with his patient, like the doctor on his ship.

MRS. SMITH   Ah! I never thought of it that way. Perhaps it's true. So what's your point?

MR. SMITH   That all doctors are quacks. And that goes for their patients too. Only the Royal Navy can be trusted in Great Britain.

MRS. SMITH   But not marines!

MR. SMITH   Indeed!

Pause.

MR. SMITH (*still reading his newspaper.*)   Something I've never understood. Given their interest in civilized society, why do newspapers always print the ages of the deceased and not the new born? It doesn't make sense!

MRS. SMITH   I never thought of it before!

Another moment of silence. The clocks strikes seven times. Silence. The clock strikes three times. Silence. The clock doesn't strike at all.

MR. SMITH (*head in the papers*)   Good grief, it says Bobby Watson died.

MRS. SMITH   My God, the poor chap, when did he die?

MR. SMITH   Why do you sound so surprised? You know perfectly well he's been dead for two years. You remember, we went to his funeral, a year and a half ago.

MRS. SMITH   Of course I remember. How could I forget? I just don't understand your surprise at reading it in the paper.

MR. SMITH   It wasn't in the paper. It's been three years since we've mentioned his death. Can't a fellow free-associate?

MRS. SMITH   What a shame! He was so well preserved.

MR. SMITH   The most smashing corpse in Great Britain! He didn't look his age. Poor Bobby, it's been four years since he died and he's still warm. A truly unruly cadaver. What a gay blade!

MRS. SMITH   Poor Bobby.

MR. SMITH   Which poor Bobby do you mean?

MRS. SMITH   Why, his wife. Like him, she was also called
Bobby, Bobby Watson. Because they had the same name,
you could never tell them apart when you saw them
together. It was only after he died that you could tell which
was which. There are still those, to this very day, who
confuse her with her dead husband and then offer their
condolences. Do you know her?

MR. SMITH   We only bumped into each other once, by
chance. At Bobby's funeral.

MRS. SMITH   I've never met her. Is she pretty?

MR. SMITH   Her features are conventional so you can't call
her a beauty. She's too tall and tubby. Her features aren't
conventional, making her a real beauty. She's a bit too small
and scrawny. She's a voice teacher.

The clock strikes five times. A long silence.

MRS. SMITH   And when do you think they'll get married?

MR. SMITH   Next spring or later.

MRS. SMITH   We'll have to go to their wedding.

MR. SMITH   And we'll have to buy them a wedding present. I
wonder what they'd like.

MRS. SMITH   Why don't we give them one of the seven
silver salad servers we got at our wedding. We've never
used them, not even once.

A brief silence. The clock strikes twice.

MRS. SMITH   It's a shame she was widowed so young.

MR. SMITH   Luckily, they didn't have children.

MRS. SMITH   That's all they would have needed! Children! The poor woman, what would she have done with them?

MR. SMITH   She's still young. Perhaps she'll remarry. Mourning becomes her.

MRS. SMITH   But then who'll take care of the children? You know perfectly well they have a son and a daughter. What are their names, again?

MR. SMITH   Bobby and Bobby, like their parents. Bobby Watson's uncle, old Bobby Watson, is rich and he dotes on the boy. He could easily foot the bill for Bobby's education.

MRS. SMITH   It's the proper thing to do. And Bobby Watson's aunt, doddery Bobby Watson, could pay for the education of Bobby Watson, the daughter of Bobby Watson. That way, Bobby Watson's mother, Bobby, would be free to remarry. Does she have anyone in mind?

MR. SMITH   Yes, one of Bobby Watson's cousins.

MRS. SMITH   Which one? Bobby Watson?

MR. SMITH   Which Bobby Watson to you mean?

MRS. SMITH   Bobby Watson, the son of old Bobby Watson, the other uncle of Bobby Watson, the deceased.

MR. SMITH   No, not him, the other one. Bobby Watson, the son of doddery Bobby Watson, the aunt of Bobby Watson, the deceased.

MRS. SMITH   Are you talking about Bobby Watson the traveling salesman?

MR. SMITH   All the Bobby Watsons are traveling salesmen!

MRS. SMITH   Tough business. One can do well, however.

MR. SMITH   Yes, when there's no competition.

MRS. SMITH   And when is there no competition?

MR. SMITH   Tuesdays, Thursdays and Tuesdays.

MRS. SMITH   Ah! Three days a week? And how does Bobby Watson spend them?

MR. SMITH   He takes it easy, he naps.

MRS. SMITH   But why doesn't he work those three days if there's no competition?

MR. SMITH   I don't know everything! I can't answer all your bloody questions!

MRS. SMITH (*hurt*)   Are you trying to humiliate me?

MR. SMITH (*all smiles*)   Who, me? Never!

MRS. SMITH   Men! You're all alike! You lie around all day, cigarette dangling from your mouth or powdering your nose and painting your lips fifty times a day—that is, if you're not drinking yourself under the table!

MR. SMITH   Well, what would you say if you saw men acting like women? Smoking all day, powdering their noses, smearing on lipstick and guzzling whiskey?

MRS. SMITH   I don't give a bloody damn! You're just trying to get my goat. I hate it when you kid around and you know it!

She throws her socks across the room and bares her teeth. She rises. *

Mr. Smith approaches her and speaks tenderly.

————

*Author's note: In the Nicolas Bataille production Mrs. Smith didn't bare her teeth or throw her socks very far.

MR. SMITH   Oh, my little guinea hen, why are you ruffling your feathers? You know I'm just teasing you. (*He takes her by the waist and kisses her.*) What a ridiculous pair of old lovebirds we are! Come, let's turn out the lights and go beddy-byes!

SCENE II

The Smiths and MARY

MARY (*entering*)   I'm the maid. I just had the most delightful afternoon. I went to the pictures with a chap and saw a film with some ladies. After the picture we stopped for a spot of brandy and milk and read the newspaper.

MRS. SMITH   I hope you had a delightful afternoon, that you went to the pictures with a chap and then stopped for a spot of brandy and milk.

MR. SMITH   Don't forget the newspaper!

MARY   Your guests, Mr. and Mrs. Martin, are at the door. They're waiting for me. They don't dare come in, unannounced. They're supposed to dine with you this evening.

MRS. SMITH   Ah yes. We were expecting them. We're starving. Since they didn't show up, we were going to eat without them. We haven't had a bite all day. You shouldn't have deserted us!

MARY   But I went with your blessing.

MR. SMITH   I wasn't thinking!

Mary bursts out laughing. Then she cries, then she smiles.

MARY   I bought myself a chamber pot!

MRS. SMITH   My dear Mary, would you be good enough to open the door and show Mr. and Mrs. Martin in? We'll change in a jiffy.

Mr. and Mrs. Smith exit to the right. Mary opens the door on the left and MR. *and* MRS. MARTIN *enter.*

SCENE III

Mary and the Martins

MARY   Why are you so late! It's extremely\rude. You're supposed to be on time. Understand? You can take a seat over there and wait.

She exits.

SCENE IV

The Martins without Mary

Mr. and Mrs. Martin sit across from each other without speaking. They exchange shy smiles. The following dialogue should be spoken in voices that are sluggish, monotonous, somewhat singsong, without nuance. ★

MR. MARTIN   Begging your pardon, dear lady, but unless I'm mistaken I feel I've met you before.

MRS. MARTIN   Me too, dear sir, I feel I've met you before.

MR. MARTIN   Could I have spotted you, dear lady, at Manchester, by any chance?

MRS. MARTIN   It's entirely possible. I'm from the city of Manchester, but I have a poor memory, dear sir, so I can't say whether we spotted each other there or not.

──────────

★Author's note: In the Nicolas Bataille production the scene was played and spoken in a sincerely tragic style.

MR. MARTIN Good God, how baffling! I'm originally from the city of Manchester too, dear lady!

MRS. MARTIN Most baffling!

MR. MARTIN Most baffling, indeed! Because I left the city of Manchester about five weeks ago, dear lady.

MRS. MARTIN How baffling! And what a bizarre coincidence! I too left the city of Manchester about five weeks ago, dear sir.

MR. MARTIN I took the 8:30 morning train that arrived in London at 4:45, dear lady.

MRS. MARTIN How baffling! How bizarre! And what a coincidence! I took the very same train, dear sir!

MR. MARTIN Good God! How baffling! Then perhaps I saw you on the train?

MRS. MARTIN It's entirely possible, it's not out of the question, it's plausible and why not? But alas, I don't remember, dear sir!

MR. MARTIN I traveled second class, dear lady. Of course there is no second class in Great Britain, but I make a point of traveling second class just the same.

MRS. MARTIN How bizarre, how baffling and what a coincidence! I too traveled second class, dear sir!

MR. MARTIN Most baffling indeed! Then perhaps we met in second class, my dear lady!

MRS. MARTIN It's possible, more than possible, but alas, I don't remember very well, my dear sir!

MR. MARTIN My seat was in coach number eight, compartment six, dear lady.

MRS. MARTIN   How baffling! My seat was also in coach number eight, compartment six, my dear sir!

MR. MARTIN   Most baffling and what a bizarre coincidence! Then perhaps we bumped into each other in compartment six, my dear lady.

MRS. MARTIN   It's entirely possible, after all! But alas, I don't remember, my dear sir!

MR. MARTIN   To tell you the truth, my dear lady, I don't remember either, but it's possible we saw each other there and if I put on my thinking cap, it seems entirely probable!

MRS. MARTIN   I say! Indeed! Well done! Jolly good, dear sir!

MR. MARTIN   How baffling! I had seat number three, next to the window, my dear lady.

MRS. MARTIN   Good God, how baffling and how bizarre! I had seat number six, next to the window, across from you, my dear sir.

MR. MARTIN   Good God, indeed! How baffling and what a coincidence! . . . Then we were sitting face-to-face, my dear lady. That is where we must have met!

MRS. MARTIN   How baffling! It is possible, but alas I don't remember, dear sir.

MR. MARTIN   To tell the truth, I don't remember either, my dear lady. However, it's entirely possible we saw each other then.

MRS. MARTIN   You've got a point, but I can't be sure, dear sir.

MR. MARTIN   Weren't you the woman, my dear lady, who asked me to lift her bag up to the luggage rack, then thanked me kindly and gave me permission to smoke?

MRS. MARTIN Of course! It must have been me, dear sir! How baffling, how very baffling, and what a coincidence!

MR. MARTIN Most baffling, bizarre and what a coincidence! So perhaps we met at that very moment, dear lady.

MRS. MARTIN How baffling and what a coincidence! It's entirely possible, my dear sir! However, I don't believe I remember.

MR. MARTIN Nor do I, dear lady.

A moment of silence.

The clock strikes twice and then once.

MR. MARTIN Since coming to London I've been living in Bromfield Street, my dear lady.

MRS. MARTIN How baffling, and how bizarre! I too have been living in Bromfield Street since coming to London, my dear sir.

MR. MARTIN How baffling, but then, but then, perhaps we met on Bromfield Street, my dear lady.

MRS. MARTIN How baffling and how bizarre! It's entirely possible after all, but alas, I don't remember, my dear sir.

MR. MARTIN I live at number 19, my dear lady.

MRS. MARTIN How baffling, I also live at number 19, my dear sir.

MR. MARTIN But then, but then, but then, but then, but then perhaps we met there, my dear lady?

MRS. MARTIN It's entirely possible, but alas, I don't remember, my dear sir.

MR. MARTIN My flat is on the fifth floor, number eight, my dear lady.

MRS. MARTIN   How baffling! My God, how bizarre! I also live on the fifth floor, in flat number eight, my dear sir!

MR. MARTIN (*thoughtfully*)   How baffling, how baffling, how baffling and what a coincidence! I have a bed in my room, you know. The bed is covered with a green duvet. This room with its bed and green duvet is at the bottom of the hall, between the library and the loo, my dear lady.

MRS. MARTIN   What a coincidence, oh my God, what a coincidence! My bedroom also has a bed covered with a green duvet and it too is at the bottom of the hall, between the library and the loo, my dear sir!

MR. MARTIN   How bizarre, baffling and beyond the pale! Then, dear lady, we live in the same room and sleep in the same bed, my dear lady. Perhaps that is where we bumped into each other.

MRS. MARTIN   How baffling and what a coincidence! It's entirely possible we met there and perchance even last night. But I don't remember, my dear sir!

MR. MARTIN   I have a little girl, my little daughter who lives with me, my dear lady. She's two years old and blonde. She has one white eye and one red eye. She's very pretty and her name is Alice, my dear lady.

MRS. MARTIN   What a bizarre coincidence! I also have a little girl who's two years old with one white eye and one red eye who's very pretty and named Alice, my dear sir!

MR. MARTIN (*in the same sluggish monotone*)   How baffling and what a coincidence! How bizarre! Perhaps they are one and the same, my dear lady!

MRS. MARTIN   Most baffling indeed! It's entirely possible, my dear sir.

A long moment of silence.

The clock then strikes twenty-nine times. Having pondered these events, Mr. Martin slowly rises, moving toward Mrs. Martin. Surprised by his solemnity, she quietly rises to meet him

MR. MARTIN (*in that same strange, singsong monotone*)   Then, my dear lady, there's no doubt we have met before and you are my lawful wife. . . . Elizabeth, at last I have found you!

Mrs. Martin slowly approaches Mr. Martin. They embrace without feeling. The clock strikes one very loud stroke. It's so loud it should make the audience jump. The Martins, however, don't hear it

MRS. MARTIN   Donald, darling, it's you!

They sit in the same chair, and fall asleep, still kissing. The clock strikes several more times. Mary quietly tiptoes into the room, her finger on her lips, and addresses the audience

SCENE V

Mr. and Mrs. Martin and Mary

MARY   Elizabeth and Donald are too over the moon to hear me, so I can let you in on a secret. Elizabeth is not Elizabeth and Donald is not Donald. And here's the proof: the little girl Donald was talking about is not Elizabeth's daughter, they're not one and the same. Donald's daughter has one white eye and one red eye, like Elizabeth's daughter, but Donald's child has a white right eye and a red left eye, whereas Elizabeth's child has a red right eye and a white left eye. So his entire argument goes up in smoke when it hits this loophole, turning his theory into dust and ashes. In spite of the extraordinary coincidences which seem rock solid, Donald and Elizabeth, not being the parents of the same child, are not Donald and Elizabeth. He can fancy

he's Donald; she can fancy she's Elizabeth. He can fancy
she's Elizabeth and she can fancy he's Donald, but both are
sadly deluded. Then who is the real Donald, you ask? And
who is the real Elizabeth? Who wants to prolong this
agony? It beats me. I say we drop the whole affair and leave
things as they are. (*taking several steps toward the door, then
facing the audience.*) In case you're interested, my real name is
Sherlock Holmes.

She exits.

SCENE VI

The Martins without Mary

*The clock strikes as often as it likes. Mr. and Mrs. Martin separate
after a few moments and return to their former seats.*

MR. MARTIN Let's forget everything that hasn't happened
between us, darling. Now that we're together, let's try not
to lose each other again and continue on our merry way.

MRS. MARTIN Yes, darling.

SCENE VII

The Martins and the Smiths

*Mr. and Mrs. Smith enter from the right without having changed their
clothes.*

MRS. SMITH Good evening, dear friends! Forgive us for
making you wait so long, but we wanted to show you the
courtesy you so richly deserve. The moment we learned
you were coming, without giving us so much as a peep of
warning, we rushed to change into black tie and tails.

MR. SMITH (*furious*)   We haven't eaten all day! You've kept us waiting for four hours. Why are you so late?

Mr. and Mrs. Smith sit facing their guests. The clock mimics the tension between them and strikes accordingly. The Martins are embarrassed and shy, particularly Mrs. Martin. Their conversation begins awkwardly. They have a hard time getting their words out. There's an agonizing silence which is followed by a string of painful lapses and hesitations.

MR. SMITH   Hm.

Silence.

MRS. SMITH   Hm, hm.

Silence.

MRS. MARTIN   Hm, hm, hm.

Silence.

MR. MARTIN   Hm, hm, hm, hm.

Silence.

MRS. MARTIN   Absolutely!

Silence.

MR. MARTIN   We all have colds.

Silence.

MR. SMITH   Yet it's not cold outside.

Silence.

MRS. SMITH   There's no draft.

Silence.

MR. MARTIN   Thank our lucky stars!

18

Silence.

MR. SMITH My oh my, oh my, oh my.

Silence.

MR. MARTIN Are you depressed?

Silence.

MRS. SMITH No, he's bored shitless.

Silence.

MRS. MARTIN Oh sir, at your age, really!

Silence.

MR. SMITH The heart is ageless.

Silence.

MR. MARTIN It's true.

Silence.

MRS. SMITH So they say.

Silence.

MRS. MARTIN They also say the opposite.

Silence.

MR. SMITH The truth lies somewhere in between.

Silence.

MR. MARTIN Right you are!

Silence.

MRS. SMITH (*to the Martins*) Since you travel so much you must have a lot of interesting stories up your sleeve.

MR. MARTIN (*to his wife*)   Tell them what you saw today, darling?

MRS. MARTIN   It's not worth it, they'd never believe me.

MR. SMITH   We wouldn't doubt you for a moment!

MRS. SMITH   You insult us if that's what you think.

MR. MARTIN (*to his wife*)   You'll insult them, if that's what you think. . . .

MRS. MARTIN (*graciously*)   All right. I saw something extraordinary today, really incredible.

MR. MARTIN   Quick, spit it out, my dear.

MR. SMITH   Ah, we're going to be entertained.

MRS. SMITH   Finally!

MRS. MARTIN   Here goes . . . While I was out shopping to buy some vegetables, which are getting increasingly dear . . .

MRS. SMITH   Where will it end?

MR. SMITH   Don't interrupt, my love. Nasty, nasty!

MRS. MARTIN   I saw a man in the street next to a café, conservatively dressed, around fifty or so who . . .

MR. SMITH   Who what?

MRS. SMITH   Who what?

MR. SMITH (*to his wife*)   Don't interrupt, my love. You're being disgusting.

MRS. SMITH   You interrupted first, my pet. You boor!

MR. MARTIN   That's enough! (*to his wife*) And what was this man doing?

MRS. MARTIN You're going to say I made it up. He was down on one knee and he was bending over.

THE OTHERS Oh!

MRS. MARTIN Yes, bending over.

MR. SMITH Impossible!

MRS. MARTIN He was bending over. I crept closer to see what he was doing. . . .

MR. SMITH And?

MRS. MARTIN He was tying his shoelace, which had come undone.

THE OTHERS Fantastic!

MR. SMITH If it hadn't come from your lips, I wouldn't believe it.

MR. MARTIN Why not? One sees much more extraordinary things out there. For example, when I was in the tube today I saw a man sitting in his seat, quietly reading the newspaper.

MRS. SMITH What an odd duck!

MR. SMITH Maybe it was the same man!

The doorbell rings.

MR. SMITH Good grief, the doorbell.

MRS. SMITH There must be someone there. I'll go and see. (*She goes to the door, opens it, peers out, then closes it and returns.*) Nobody.

She sits back down.

MR. MARTIN Let me give you another example. . . .

The doorbell rings.

MR. SMITH   Good grief, the doorbell.

MRS. SMITH   There must be someone there. I'll go and see. (*She goes to the door, opens it, peers out, then closes it and returns.*) Nobody.

She sits back down.

MR. MARTIN (*struggling to remember where he was*)   Uh, uh, uh . . .

MRS. MARTIN   You said you were going to give us another example.

MR. MARTIN   Ah yes!

The doorbell rings.

MR. SMITH   Good grief, the doorbell.

MRS. SMITH   I'm not going to answer it.

MR. SMITH   Yes, but someone must be there!

MRS. SMITH   The first time there was nobody. The second time, nobody. What makes you think someone's there now?

MR. SMITH   Because they rang!

MRS. MARTIN   That's no reason.

MR. MARTIN   What are you talking about? When you hear the doorbell ring, it means someone's at the door. They rang so you'd let them in.

MRS. MARTIN   Not always, as you just saw.

MR. MARTIN   But in most cases, yes.

MR. SMITH   Whenever I visit someone, I ring the bell to get in. It's what people do! When the doorbell rings, it means someone's there!

MRS. SMITH   It's true in theory. But in reality, things are different, as you just saw.

MRS. MARTIN   Your wife is right.

MR. MARTIN   Oh, you women! You're always sticking up for each other.

MRS. SMITH   All right, I'll go check again. You can't say I'm not game, but you'll see, no one will be there! (*She goes to the door, peers out and closes it.*) What did I tell you? Nobody. (*She returns to her seat.*)

MRS. MARTIN   Ah men! They always think they're right, and they're always wrong!

The doorbell rings.

MR. SMITH   Good grief, the doorbell. Someone must be there.

MRS. SMITH (*in a fit of rage*)   Don't send me to that bloody door again! As you've seen it's pointless! We've learned from experience that whenever you hear the doorbell ring, no one's ever there.

MRS. MARTIN   Never.

MR. MARTIN   That's not always true.

MR. SMITH   In fact, it's false! Usually when you hear the doorbell, it means someone is there.

MRS. SMITH   He can't admit he's wrong.

MRS. MARTIN   My husband is pigheaded too.

MR. SMITH   Someone is there.

23

MR. MARTIN   It's not impossible.

MRS. SMITH (*to her husband*)   No.

MR. SMITH   Yes.

MRS. SMITH   I said, no! In any case, you're not going to bother me again for nothing. If you want to make sure, go see for yourself!

MR. SMITH   I'm going.

Mrs. Smith shrugs her shoulders. Mrs. Martin nods her head

MR. SMITH ★(*opening the door*)   Tiens! *Je suis enchanté de vous voir!* (*glancing at the others, who look surprised*) It's the Fire Captain!

SCENE VIII

The Smiths, the Martins and the FIRE CAPTAIN

THE FIRE CAPTAIN (*in uniform, of course, wearing an enormous shiny helmet*)   Good day, ladies and gentlemen.

They gape at him, astonished. Mrs. Smith is furious and looks away, refusing to acknowledge him.

THE FIRE CAPTAIN   Good day, Mrs. Smith, you seem angry.

MRS. SMITH   Oh!

MR. SMITH   As you see, my wife is a bit miffed at having been proved wrong.

MR. MARTIN   There's been a running argument between Mr. and Mrs. Smith, Captain.

★Translator's note: Whenever the dialogue appears in English, it's translated into French.

MRS. SMITH (*to Mr. Martin*) It's none of your business! (*to Mr. Smith*) How many times do I have to tell you not to drag strangers into our family squabbles!

MR. SMITH Calm down, my pet, it's not serious. The Fire Captain is an old friend of the family's. His mother courted me and I knew his father. He wanted to marry my daughter if I ever had one. And he died waiting.

MR. MARTIN It's neither his fault, nor yours.

THE FIRE CAPTAIN All right, what's going on?

MRS. SMITH My husband was claiming . . .

MR. SMITH No, it was you who were claiming . . .

MR. MARTIN Yes, it was her.

MRS. MARTIN No, it was him.

THE FIRE CAPTAIN Don't get your knickers in a twist. Just tell me what happened, Mrs. Smith.

MRS. SMITH All right, here goes. I'm a bit wary of letting my hair down with you, but then again a fireman is also a confessor.

THE FIRE CAPTAIN Go on.

MRS. SMITH We were arguing because my husband said whenever you hear the doorbell ring, there's always someone there.

MR. MARTIN It's plausible.

MRS. SMITH And I said, every time you hear the doorbell ring, no one is there.

MRS. MARTIN It might seem strange.

MRS. SMITH   But it's been proven. Not by theoretical woolgathering, but by hard facts.

MR. SMITH   Not true, because the Fire Captain is here. He rang the bell, I opened the door and there he was.

MRS. MARTIN   When?

MR. MARTIN   Just now.

MRS. SMITH   Yes, but it was only after hearing it ring four times that you found someone there. And the fourth time doesn't count.

MRS. MARTIN   Exactly! Only the first three times count.

MR. SMITH   Let me ask you a few questions, Captain.

THE FIRE CAPTAIN   Be my guest.

MR. SMITH   When I opened the door and saw you, was it you who had rung the bell?

THE FIRE CAPTAIN   Yes, it was me.

MR. MARTIN   You were at the door. And you rang to get in.

THE FIRE CAPTAIN   I can't deny it.

MR. SMITH (*to his wife, victoriously*)   You see? I was right! When you hear the doorbell, it's because somebody is there. And you can't claim the Fire Captain's not somebody!

MRS. SMITH   Certainly not. But let me repeat I was only speaking about the first three times because the fourth one doesn't count.

MRS. MARTIN   And when the doorbell rang the first time, was it you?

THE FIRE CAPTAIN   No, it wasn't me.

MRS. MARTIN   You see? The doorbell rang and no one was there.

MR. MARTIN   Perhaps it was someone else?

MR. SMITH   Were you at the door a long time?

THE FIRE CAPTAIN   Three quarters of an hour.

MR. SMITH   And you saw no one?

THE FIRE CAPTAIN   Nobody. I'm sure.

MRS. MARTIN   Did you hear the doorbell ring the second time?

THE FIRE CAPTAIN   Yes, but that wasn't me either. Nobody was ever there.

MRS. SMITH   Victory! I was right!

MR. SMITH (*to his wife*)   Not so fast. (*to the Fire Captain*) And what were you doing at the door?

THE FIRE CAPTAIN   Nothing. I was taking it easy. I had a lot on my mind.

MR. MARTIN   But the third time, wasn't that you who rang?

THE FIRE CAPTAIN   Yes, it was me.

MR. SMITH   But when we opened the door, we didn't see you.

THE FIRE CAPTAIN   That's because I was hiding. I was playing a joke.

MRS. SMITH   This isn't a laughing matter, Captain. It's a very sad affair.

MR. MARTIN   Nevertheless when the doorbell rings, we still don't know whether someone is there or not.

MRS. SMITH   Never anyone.

MR. SMITH   Always someone.

THE FIRE CAPTAIN   I'm going to settle it once and for all. You're both partially right. When the doorbell rings, sometimes someone is there and other times no one is there.

MR. MARTIN   It seems logical to me.

MRS. MARTIN   Me too.

THE FIRE CAPTAIN   Actually, it's all very simple. (*to the Smiths*) Go on, kiss and make up.

MRS. SMITH   We just kissed a little while ago.

MR. MARTIN   They'll kiss tomorrow. They have plenty of time.

MRS. SMITH   Now that you've helped us shed light on all this, make yourself comfortable, Captain. Take off your helmet and sit down for a minute.

THE FIRE CAPTAIN   Forgive me, but I can't stay long. I'd like to take off my helmet, but I don't have time to sit down. (*He sits down but doesn't take off his helmet.*) I have to confess I came for other reasons. I'm on official business.

MRS. SMITH   And what can we do for you, Captain?

THE FIRE CAPTAIN   I beg you to forgive my impudence. . . . (*stricken with embarrassment*) My uh . . . uh . . . (*pointing to the Martins*) May I . . . I mean, in front of them . . .

MRS. MARTIN   Feel free.

MR. MARTIN We're old friends. We tell each other everything.

MR. SMITH Carry on.

THE FIRE CAPTAIN All right, here goes. Is there a fire here?

MRS. SMITH Why do you ask?

THE FIRE CAPTAIN Because . . . begging your pardon . . . because I have orders to extinguish all fires in the city.

MRS. MARTIN All of them?

THE FIRE CAPTAIN Yes, each and every one.

MRS. SMITH (*confused*) I don't know. . . . I don't think so. Would you care to have a look around?

MR. SMITH (*sniffing the air*) There can't be one here. I don't smell anything burning.★

THE FIRE CAPTAIN (*upset*) Nothing at all? A small chimney fire? Something smoldering in the attic or basement? A few sparks starting to fly?

MRS. SMITH Listen, I don't want to disappoint you, but I'm afraid we have nothing at the moment. I promise to let you know the moment we do.

THE FIRE CAPTAIN Don't forget! It would be a big help.

MRS. SMITH It's a promise.

THE FIRE CAPTAIN (*to the Martins*) And nothing's burning at your house either?

MRS. MARTIN Alas, no.

★Author's note: in the Nicolas Bataille production Mr. and Mrs. Martin sniffed as well.

MR. MARTIN (*to the Fire Captain*)   Things are looking pretty grim.

THE FIRE CAPTAIN   Grim and grimmer. There's nothing out there, just chicken feed—a chimney here, a barn there. Nothing big. It doesn't bring anything in. Because there's no yield, the profits on returns are negligible.

MR. SMITH   Times are tough. It's the same everywhere. Business, agriculture . . . It's like your fires this year, nothing's happening.

MR. MARTIN   No wheat, no fires.

THE FIRE CAPTAIN   No floods either.

MRS. SMITH   But we have sugar.

MR. SMITH   Because it's imported.

MRS. MARTIN   Fires are trickier. Taxes are sky high.

THE FIRE CAPTAIN   Please! There's an occasional asphyxiation by gas but it's rare. A young woman asphyxiated herself last week because she left the gas on.

MRS. MARTIN   She forgot to turn it off?

THE FIRE CAPTAIN   No, she thought it was her peignoir.

MR. SMITH   These mix-ups are always dangerous!

MRS. SMITH   Did you call on the match maker?

THE FIRE CAPTAIN   Nothing doing! He's insured against fire.

MR. MARTIN   Feel free to visit the Vicar of Wakefield and use my name.

THE FIRE CAPTAIN   I don't have the jurisdiction to put out fires set by priests. The Bishop would get angry. They put out their own fires or else have them extinguished by vestal virgins.

MR. SMITH   Try and contact the Durands.

THE FIRE CAPTAIN   I can't do that either. He's not British. He's only naturalized. Naturalized citizens have the right to own houses, but not to save them if they catch fire.

MRS. SMITH   Yet when a house went up in flames last year, it was extinguished just the same!

THE FIRE CAPTAIN   They took care of it by themselves. Under cover of night. Don't look at me, I wouldn't breathe a word.

MR. SMITH   Me either.

MRS. SMITH   Since you have time on your hands, stay a bit longer, Captain. It would give us such pleasure.

THE FIRE CAPTAIN   Would you like me to tell you some stories?

MRS. SMITH   Oh, please do! You're charming.

She kisses him.

THE OTHERS   Yes, yes! Stories! Bravo!

They applaud.

MR. SMITH   What makes them so interesting is firemen's stories are always true. They've been lived.

THE FIRE CAPTAIN   I only talk about my own experience. The truth, the whole truth and nothing but the truth. No fiction.

MR. MARTIN   That's right. Truth isn't found in books, only in life.

MRS. SMITH   Begin!

MR. MARTIN   Begin!

MRS. MARTIN   Shhhh! He's beginning.

THE FIRE CAPTAIN (*coughing a few times*)   Please! Don't look at me that way. You're embarrassing me. You know I'm shy.

MRS. SMITH   Isn't he charming?

She kisses him again.

THE FIRE CAPTAIN   All right, I'll try to start again, but promise you won't listen.

MRS. MARTIN   But if we don't listen, we won't be able to hear you.

THE FIRE CAPTAIN   I hadn't thought of that!

MRS. SMITH   I told you. He's just a boy.

MR. MARTIN and **MR. SMITH**   Oh, the dear child.

They kiss him. ★

MRS. MARTIN   Stiff upper lip!

THE FIRE CAPTAIN   All right, here goes. (*coughing a few more times, then speaking in a voice trembling with emotion*) "The Dog and the Ox," an experimental fable. Once upon a time, another ox asked another dog, "Why haven't you swallowed your trunk?" "Forgive me," replied the dog, "It's because I thought I was an elephant."

MRS. MARTIN   And what's the moral?

★Author's note: In the Nicolas Bataille production Mr. Martin and Mr. Smith did not kiss him.

THE FIRE CAPTAIN   That's for you to sort out.

MR. SMITH   He's right.

MRS. SMITH (*furious*)   Tell us another!

THE FIRE CAPTAIN   A young calf ate too much ground glass. As a result he had to give birth. A cow was born. Because the calf was male, this cow couldn't call him "Mother." And she certainly couldn't call him "Father" because he was too young. The calf was then obliged to get married to someone so the county clerk made every effort to dot his i's and cross his t's.

MR. SMITH   ★How do you cross a t?

MR. MARTIN   With a stroke.

THE FIRE CAPTAIN   But if he has a stroke, he'll die.

MRS. SMITH   Poor thing.

MRS. MARTIN   I can't dot my T's, but I can cross my eyes. Look! (*She crosses them.*)

Everyone gasps, then silence.

FIRE CAPTAIN   I'll tell you another one. "The Cock." Once upon a time there was a cock who wanted to play the dog. But he didn't have a chance because he was recognized right away.

MRS. SMITH   On the other hand, the dog who wanted to play the cock was never recognized.

MR. SMITH   Now it's my turn. I want to tell one. "The Snake and the Fox." Once upon a time a snake approached a fox

---

★Translator's note: Since the Smiths and Martins wouldn't indulge in French wordplay, this is a British rendering of their exchange.

33

and said, "I think I know you!" The fox replied, "I think I know you too." "Then hand over some money," the snake said. "But a fox doesn't handle money," replied the clever creature, who beat a hasty retreat by jumping into a deep valley full of strawberries and apiaries. The snake was waiting for him, however, laughing a Mephistophelian laugh. The fox pulled out his knife, yelling, "I'm going to teach you how to live!" at which point he turned tail and fled. But he didn't have a prayer. The snake was quicker. With a well-chosen blow, he hit the fox smack in the forehead which, then broke into a thousand pieces as he cried, "No! No! No! No! No! No! I am not your daughter!"★

MRS. MARTIN   Interesting.

MRS. SMITH   Not bad.

MR. MARTIN (*shaking Mr. Smith's hand*)   My congratulations.

THE FIRE CAPTAIN (*jealous*)   It wasn't so great. Plus I'd heard it before.

MR. SMITH   It was terrible.

MRS. SMITH   It wasn't even true.

MRS. MARTIN   But alas, it was.

MR. MARTIN (*to Mrs. Smith*)   And now it's your turn, dear lady.

MRS. SMITH   I only know one. Here goes. It's called, "The Bouquet."

MR. SMITH   My wife has always been a romantic.

★Author's note: In the Nicolas Bataille production Mr. Smith mimed this speech without saying a word.

MR. MARTIN   A dyed-in-the-wool Englishwoman!*

MRS. SMITH   All right! Once upon a time a man gave his fiancée a bouquet. She said "Thank you," but before she could get the words out of her mouth, he snatched it back to teach her a lesson, saying, "Hand it over!" Then he bid her farewell, tucked it under his arm and disappeared over the horizon.

MR. MARTIN   Charming!

He might kiss Mrs. Smith or not.

MRS. MARTIN   Mr. Smith, you have a wife who makes us green with envy.

MR. SMITH   It's true, my wife is intelligence personified. She's far more intelligent than I am. She's also more feminine. Or so they say.

MRS. SMITH   Tell us another, Captain.

THE FIRE CAPTAIN   No, it's getting late.

MR. MARTIN   Tell us one anyway.

THE FIRE CAPTAIN   I'm too tired.

MR. SMITH   Come on, be a good egg.

MR. MARTIN   Please?

THE FIRE CAPTAIN   No.

MRS. MARTIN   You have a heart of ice. We're sitting on hot coals!

---

*Author's note: In the Nicolas Bataille production these two phrases were repeated three times.

MRS. SMITH (*falling to her knees, sobbing, or not*) I'm begging you!

THE FIRE CAPTAIN If you insist.

MR. SMITH (*in Mrs. Martin's ear*) He agreed! He's going to bore us again.

MRS. MARTIN Bloody hell!

MRS. SMITH Just my luck. I was too polite.

THE FIRE CAPTAIN "The head cold": My brother-in-law on my father's side had a first cousin whose maternal uncle had a father-in-law whose paternal grandfather had taken an aborigine as his second wife, a young woman whose brother he met on his travels, a girl he was mad about, with whom he had a son who married a fearless female pharmacist who was none other than the niece of an unknown fourth-class petty officer of the Royal Navy whose adoptive father had an aunt who spoke fluent Spanish, who might have been one of the granddaughters of an electrical engineer who died young, who was himself the owner of a vineyard which produced second-rate wine, but who had a second cousin, an agoraphobic, a sergeant-major whose son had married a bombshell, a divorcée, whose first husband was the son of a loyal patriot, who, eager to strike it rich, raised one of his daughters to marry a big game hunter who knew Rothschild, whose brother, after flitting from one job to another, married, and had a daughter whose great-grandfather, a midget, wore spectacles which were given to him by one of his cousins, the brother-in-law of a Portuguese, if you please—the natural son of a pastry chef who was pretty well-off, whose foster brother married the daughter of a former country doctor who was himself the foster brother of the son of a dairy farmer who happened to

36

be the natural son of another country doctor, married three times in a row, whose third wife . . .

MR. MARTIN   I knew his third wife, if I'm not mistaken. She dined on roast chicken in a hornet's nest.

THE FIRE CAPTAIN   It's not the same one.

MRS. SMITH   Settle down!

THE FIRE CAPTAIN   As I was saying . . . whose third wife was the daughter of the best midwife in the area who was widowed before her time . . .

MR. SMITH   Like my wife.

THE FIRE CAPTAIN   . . . who remarried a glass blower with get-up-and-go, who had a child with the daughter of a stationmaster, who tripped the light fantastic . . .

MRS. SMITH   Turned to feats gymnastic . . .

MR. MARTIN   Then took his vows monastic . . .

THE FIRE CAPTAIN   Having married a greengrocer whose father had a brother, mayor of a small village, married to a blonde nursery school teacher whose cousin, a fly fisherman . . .

MR. MARTIN   A fly on the wall?

THE FIRE CAPTAIN   . . . had wed another blonde nursery school teacher, also named Marie whose brother was married to a Marie as well, who also happened to be a blonde nursery school teacher . . .

MR. SMITH   Because she's blonde, she must be Marie.

THE FIRE CAPTAIN   . . . whose father had been raised in Canada by an old woman who was the niece of a priest whose grandmother, like everyone else in the winter, sometimes caught a cold.

MRS. SMITH   A curious tale. Almost unbelievable.

MR. MARTIN   If you catch cold, you must wrap it up.

MR. SMITH   It's a useless precaution, but absolutely necessary.

MRS. MARTIN   Excuse me, Captain, but I didn't completely understand your story. When you got to the grandmother of the priest at the end, I got confused.

MR. SMITH   One always gets confused in the hands of a priest.

MRS. SMITH   Begin again, Captain! We beg of you.

THE FIRE CAPTAIN   Ah! I don't know if I can. I'm on duty. It depends on what time it is.

MRS. SMITH   We don't have the correct time, here.

THE FIRE CAPTAIN   But what about the clock?

MR. SMITH   It doesn't run well. It has a wayward streak. When it strikes, the hour is always the opposite of what it's supposed to be.

SCENE IX

The Smiths, the Martins, the Fire Captain and Mary

MARY (*entering*)   Ma'am, sir . . .

MRS. SMITH   What do you want?

MR. SMITH   Why are you barging in here?

MARY   Please excuse me, ma'am, sir and assorted ladies and gentlemen, but I would like . . . I would also like to tell a story.

38

MRS. MARTIN   What is she saying?

MR. MARTIN   I think our friends' maid has flipped her lid. She also wants to tell a story.

THE FIRE CAPTAIN   Who does she think she is? (*looking at her*) Oh!

MRS. SMITH   Why are you meddling in our affairs?

MR. SMITH   You're out of bounds, Mary.

THE FIRE CAPTAIN   Oh, but it's her! Impossible!

MR. SMITH   You too?

MARY   Impossible! Here?

MRS. SMITH   What is the meaning of this?

MR. SMITH   You know each other?

THE FIRE CAPTAIN   Do we ever!

Mary throws herself at the Fire Captain. They're all over each other.

MARY   I'm so happy to see you again. . . . At last!

MR. and **MRS. SMITH**   Oh!

MR. SMITH   This is too much, in our home, here in the outskirts of London.

MRS. SMITH   It's most inappropriate!

THE FIRE CAPTAIN   She doused my very first flames.

MARY   I'm his wet little water spout.

MR. MARTIN   If this is the case, dear friends . . . these feelings are understandable, human, even honorable. . . .

MRS. MARTIN   All that is human is honorable.

39

MRS. SMITH   Still, I don't like to see this sort of behavior here . . . among us.

MR. SMITH   She wasn't properly raised. . . .

THE FIRE CAPTAIN   Oh, you're too prejudiced.

MRS. MARTIN   Even though it's none of my business, I think a maid is never anything but a maid.

MR. MARTIN   Even if she can pass for a good detective.

THE FIRE CAPTAIN   Give me a break.

MARY   Relax! They're not all that bad.

MR. SMITH   Hmmm . . . hmmmm . . . You two are very sweet together, but still a touch, a touch . . .

MR. MARTIN   Yes, that's that right word.

MR. SMITH   A touch too much.

MR. MARTIN   Excuse me for thinking out loud again, but there's an innate British reserve, not understood by foreigners, even specialists, thanks to whom . . . if I may speak frankly . . . I'm not referring to you, of course. . . .

MARY   Just let me tell you one tiny . . .

MR. SMITH   Not a word . . .

MARY   But I must!

MRS. SMITH   Go, my little Mary . . . go quietly into the kitchen and read your poems in front of the mirror. . . .

MR. MARTIN   I say! Even though I'm not a maid I also read poems in front of the mirror.

MRS. MARTIN   When you looked in the mirror this morning, you didn't see yourself.

MR. MARTIN That's because I wasn't there yet. . . .

MARY Could I just recite one teensy-weensy poem for you?

MRS. SMITH My little Mary, you're as stubborn as dirt!

MARY I'm going to recite a poem then, it's settled. The
poem is titled "The Fire" in honor of the Fire Captain.
"The Fire"
The polycanders were burning in the woods
A stone caught fire
The castle caught fire
The forest caught fire
The men caught fire
The women caught fire
The birds caught fire
The fish caught fire
The water caught fire
The sky caught fire
The ashes caught fire
The smoke caught fire
The fire caught fire
Everything caught fire
Caught fire, caught fire, caught fire . . . etc.

She keeps reciting the poem as the Smiths push her offstage.

SCENE X

The Smiths, the Martins and the Fire Captain without Mary

MRS. MARTIN That sent chills down my spine. . . .

MR. MARTIN It had a certain warmth, however. . . .

THE FIRE CAPTAIN I thought it was first-rate.

MRS. SMITH Just the same . . .

MR. SMITH   You exaggerate. . . .

THE FIRE CAPTAIN   Listen, it's true . . . it's all highly subjective . . . but it's my view of the world. My dream. My ideal. Which reminds me, I have to go now. Since you don't have the correct time, in exactly three quarters of an hour and sixteen minutes, I have a fire on the other side of town. I've got to get a wiggle on even though it won't amount to much.

MRS. SMITH   What will it be? A little chimney fire?

THE FIRE CAPTAIN   Not even. A smoking grate and a touch of heartburn.

MR. SMITH   Well, we're sorry to see you go.

MRS. SMITH   You've been most entertaining.

MRS. MARTIN   Thanks to you, we've passed a thoroughly Cartesian quarter of an hour.

THE FIRE CAPTAIN (*going toward the door, then stopping*) Since we're on the subject, what do you make of the bald soprano?

A general embarrassed silence.

MRS. SMITH   She always styles her hair the same way!

THE FIRE CAPTAIN   Ah! Then I bid you farewell. . . . Gentlemen . . . Ladies.

MR. MARTIN   Good luck and good fire!

THE FIRE CAPTAIN   Let's hope so. For everyone's sake.

The Fire Captain exits. They see him to the door and then return to their seats.

scene XI

The Smiths and the Martins without the Fire Captain

MRS. MARTIN I can buy a pocketknife for my brother, but you can't buy Ireland for your grandfather.

MR. SMITH We walk with our feet, but stay warm with electricity or coal.

MRS. MARTIN Sell a bull today and tomorrow you'll have wool.

MRS. SMITH One must look out the window in life.

MRS. MARTIN We can sit in a chair, even if the chair doesn't have any.

MR. SMITH Leave no stone unturned.

MR. MARTIN The ceiling is above, the floor is below.

MRS. SMITH When I say yes, it's a figure of speech.

MRS. MARTIN To each his own.

MR. SMITH Take a circle, caress it and it will become a vicious circle.

MRS. SMITH A schoolmaster teaches children how to read, but a cat suckles its kittens when they're young.

MRS. MARTIN Cows, however, turn on their tails.

MR. SMITH When I'm in the country I love the solitude and quiet.

MR. MARTIN You're not old enough for that yet!

MRS. SMITH Benjamin Franklin was right: you're less relaxed than he is.

MRS. MARTIN What are the seven days of the week?

MR. SMITH   *Lundi, Mardi, Mercredi, Jeudi, Vendredi, Samedi, Dimanche.*

MR. MARTIN   *Edouard est employé de banque, sa soeur Nanette est secrétaire et son frère Guillaume est vendeur.*

MRS. SMITH   What a funny family!

MRS. MARTIN   I prefer a bird in the bush to a sock in a clock.

MR. SMITH   Don't bear malice toward Alice, drink milk in the palace!

MR. MARTIN   An Englishman's home is his true palace.

MRS. SMITH   I don't know enough Spanish to be understood.

MRS. MARTIN   I'll give you my mother-in-law's basket if you give me your husband's casket.

MR. SMITH   I'm looking for a monophysite priest to marry our maid.

MR. MARTIN   Bread is a tree whereas bread is also a tree and an oak gives birth to another oak every single morning at the crack of dawn.

MRS. SMITH   My uncle lives in the country, but that's none of the midwife's business.

MR. MARTIN   Paper is for writing, cats are for rats and cheese is for scratching.

MRS. SMITH   Cars go fast, but the cook beats better batter.

MR. SMITH   Don't be duped, kiss the collaborator.

MR. MARTIN   *Charité bien ordonnée commence par soi-même.*

MRS. SMITH   I'm waiting for the aqueduct to drop by at my windmill.

MR. MARTIN   It can be proved that social progress is better sprinkled with sugar.

MR. SMITH   Down with shoe polish!

The others fall into a stupefied silence after Mr. Smith's outburst. Nerves are on edge. The striking of the clock mimics their agitation. The speeches that follow should start with a glacial hostility that keeps building. By the end of the scene the four of them should be standing cheek by jowl, fists raised and screaming, on the verge of tearing each other to bits.

MR. MARTIN   You mustn't polish spectacles with black shoe polish.

MRS. SMITH   Yes, but money buys you anything you want.

MR. MARTIN   I'd rather kill a rabbit than break a nasty habit.

MR. SMITH   Cockatoos, cockatoos, cockatoos, cockatoos, cockatoos, cockatoos, cockatoos, cockatoos, cockatoos, cockatoos.

MRS. SMITH   What a caa-caaphony, what a caa-caaphony, what a caa-caaphony, what a caa-caaphony, what a caa-caaphony, what a caa-caaphony, what a caa-caaphony, what a caa-caaphony, what a caa-caaphony.

MR. MARTIN   Cascades of caa-caa, cascades of caa-caa, cascades of caa-caa, cascades of caa-caa, cascades of caa-caa, cascades of caa-caa, cascades of caa-caa, cascades of caa-caa.

MR. SMITH   Dogs have fleas, dogs have fleas.

MRS. MARTIN   Cactus! Coccyx! Crocus! Coxcomb! Cockroach!

MRS. SMITH   Caa-caafier, you have made caa-caa all over us.

MR. MARTIN   I'd rather lay an egg than live in Winnipeg!

45

MRS. MARTIN (*opening her mouth very wide*)   Ah! Oh! Ah ! Oh! I must gnash my teeth.

MR. SMITH   Crocodile!

MR. MARTIN   Let's go slap Ulysses in the face!

MR. SMITH   I'm going to live in my cabana under my caa-caa trees.

MRS. MARTIN   Caa-caa trees in caa-caa groves don't bear coconuts but caa-caa nuts! Caa-caa trees in caa-caa groves don't bear coconuts but caa-caa nuts! Caa-caa trees in caa-caa groves don't bear coconuts but caa-caa nuts!

MRS. SMITH   Bats have bushy brows, but bushy brows aren't bats.

MRS. MARTIN   Don't flip my slippers.★

MR. MARTIN   Slip me my flippers!

MR. SMITH   Ship out the skippers, but don't tip the strippers.

MRS. MARTIN   Bring on the kippers.

MRS. SMITH   Zip up my knickers!

MR. MARTIN   Whip the tripper, trip the whipper!

MR. SMITH   Clip the snipper!

MRS. MARTIN   Jack the Ripper!

MRS. SMITH   You're quite the quipper!

MR. MARTIN   We're all feeling chipper!

MR. SMITH   Stiff upper lipper!

★Translator's note: Once again this is a British rendering of a thoroughly French outburst.

MRS. MARTIN Saint Nitouche touched my slipper.

MRS. SMITH Don't touch it, it's broken.

MR. MARTIN James!

MR. SMITH Boswell!

MRS. MARTIN and **MR. SMITH** Edith!

MRS. SMITH and **MR. MARTIN** Sitwell!

MRS. MARTIN and **MR. SMITH** George!

MRS. SMITH and **MR. MARTIN** Orwell!

MRS. MARTIN Gooey gurgles galore, gooey gurgles galore!

MR. MARTIN Marietta, mind your pots!

MRS. SMITH Hare Krishna! Hare Krishna! Hare Krishna!

MR. SMITH The pope eloped. The pope's no dope. It's not a joke, but a slippery slope.

MRS. MARTIN Byron, Browning, Beowulf!

MR. MARTIN Bizarre, baroque, brassiere!

MR. SMITH A,e,i,o,u; a,e,i,o,u; a,e,i,o,u!

MRS. MARTIN B,c,d,f,g,l,m,n,p,r,s,t,v,w,x,z!

MR. MARTIN Ale has oil, but kale can't boil.

MRS. SMITH (*imitating a train*) Choo choo choo choo choo choo choo choo choo choo, choo!

MR. SMITH Don't!

MRS. MARTIN Say!

MR. MARTIN They're!

MRS. SMITH There!

MR. SMITH I!

MRS. MARTIN Hear!

MR. MARTIN They're!

MRS. SMITH Here!

At the height of their fury, they all start screaming in each other's ears. The lights go off. In the darkness the rhythm of their cries picks up speed.

ALL Don't say they're there, I hear they're here;
    don't say they're there, I hear they're here;
    don't say they're there, I hear they're here;
    don't say they're there, I hear they're here;
    don't say they're there, I hear they're here;
    don't say they're there, I hear they're here!★

They stop abruptly. The lights return. Mr. and Mrs. Martin are sitting like the Smiths at the beginning of the play. They start reciting the Smiths' lines as the curtain slowly falls.

CURTAIN

★Author's note: In the Nicolas Bataille production some of these responses in the last scene were cut or transposed. It was after the hundredth performance of *The Bald Soprano* that the author had the brilliant idea of starting the play over again with Mr. and Mrs. Martin playing the roles of Mr. and Mrs. Smith.

THE LESSON
A COMIC DRAMA

The Lesson premiered at the Théatre de Pôche on February 20, 1951 under the direction of Marcel Cuvelier, who also played the role of The Professor.

THE CHARACTERS

THE PROFESSOR 50 to 60   Marvel Cuvelier
THE STUDENT 18   Rosette Zuchelli
THE MAID 45 to 50   Claude Mansard

The translation of *The Lesson* by Tina Howe had its World Premiere on September 19, 2004 at Atlantic Theater Company: Neil Pepe, Artistic Director; Andrew D. Hamingson, Managing Director; Melinda Berk, General Manager; Kurt Gardner, Production Manager; Boneau/Bryan-Brown, Press Representative. Set design was by Loy Arcenas; costume design by Theresa Squire; lighting design by Josh Bradford; sound design by Obadiah Eaves; dramaturge, Christian Parker; casting, Bernard Telsey Casting; fight director, Rick Sordelet; and production stage manager, Jennifer Grutza. Directed by Carl Forsman. The cast was as follows:

THE MAID   Christa Scott-Reed
THE PROFESSOR   Steven Skybell
THE STUDENT   Maggie Kiley

The old professor's office/dining room. Stage left, a door leads to a staircase, another door leads to a hall upstage right. There's a small window with plain curtains upstage left with the usual flowering plants on the windowsill. One can see a little town with low buildings and red roofs in the distance. The sky is blue-gray. There's a rustic table stage right and a table that doubles as a desk, center stage. Three chairs are around it with two others on either side of the window. The wallpaper is pale and there are a few bookshelves. The curtain rises. Nothing happens for several moments, then the doorbell rings.

VOICE OF THE MAID (*from the hall*)   Yes. I'm coming.

THE MAID *is heard running down the stairs. She's a big woman between forty-five and fifty. She has a ruddy complexion and wears a peasant cap. She rushes in like a gust of wind, slamming the door to the right. She dries her hands on her apron as she runs toward the door on the left. The bell rings again.*

THE MAID   Just a minute! I'm coming!

She opens the door. The young STUDENT enters, age eighteen. Gray apron, small white collar, carrying a briefcase under her arm.

THE MAID   Good morning, Mademoiselle.

THE STUDENT   Good morning, Madame. Is the Professor home?

THE MAID   Are you here for your lesson?

THE STUDENT   Yes, Madame.

THE MAID   He's expecting you. Sit down a minute, I'll tell him you're here.

THE STUDENT   Thank you, Madame.

She sits near the table, facing the audience, her back to the door on the right, through which the Maid rushes out

THE MAID (*voice raised*)   Professor, come downstairs, please. Your student is here.

VOICE OF THE PROFESSOR (*thin and strained*)   Thank you. I'm coming. . . . Give me two minutes. . . .

The Maid exits. The Student primly settles into a chair to wait, adjusting her legs just so, briefcase on her knees. She glances around the room, looking at the furniture and up at the ceiling. Then she takes a notebook out of her briefcase, leafs through it and pauses at a page to review a lesson in a last-ditch attempt to memorize it. She seems well brought up and polite, full of fun and life, with a fresh smile on her lips. In the course of the play she gradually loses her buoyancy, becoming increasingly sad and morose. Carefree and smiling at the outset, she becomes more and more exhausted, withdrawn and somnolent. Toward the end of the play, her face should be suffused with nervous depression which is reflected in her speech. Her tongue becomes heavy and she has an increasingly hard time remembering words. She speaks with difficulty and seems vaguely paralyzed, in the beginning stages of aphasia. Self-confident and strong, almost aggressive at the start, she becomes increasingly passive until she's almost a mute inanimate object in the Professor's hands—so much so that when he makes his final gesture, she doesn't react. Deadened, her reflexes are gone. Only her eyes reveal unspeakable astonishment and fear in her otherwise blank face. These changes in behavior should occur imperceptibly.

THE PROFESSOR *enters. He's a little old man with a pointed white beard. He wears a pince-nez, a black skullcap, a long black schoolmaster's gown, black trousers and black shoes, a detachable white collar and black tie. He's excessively polite and very timid, his voice deadened by this timidity. He's exceedingly correct, very much the professor. He keeps rubbing his hands together. From time to time he gets a lewd gleam in his eye which he quickly suppresses.*

In the course of the play, his timidity gradually disappears and his lewd glances become a steady devouring flame. Harmless at the outset, the Professor becomes more and more sure of himself—nervous, aggressive and dominating—until he controls the Student, who becomes helpless in his hands. Naturally, his voice, which was thin and reedy at the beginning, becomes stronger and stronger until it rings out like a clarion call, whereas the Student's voice becomes virtually inaudible after having been so clear and true at the start. In the opening scenes the Professor might have a slight stutter.

THE PROFESSOR Good morning, Mademoiselle . . . It's you, it's really you, isn't it? My new student?

THE STUDENT (*Turning quickly in a lively self-possessed way, a young woman of the world, she rises to meet him with her hand extended.*) Yes, Professor. Good morning, Professor. As you see, I'm on time. I didn't want to be late.

THE PROFESSOR That's good, Mademoiselle. Thank you. But you didn't have to rush. I can't forgive myself for making you wait. I was just finishing . . . that is to say . . . I'm so sorry. . . . You will excuse me, won't you?

THE STUDENT For what, Professor? There's no harm done, Professor.

THE PROFESSOR I'm so sorry. Did you have trouble finding the place?

THE STUDENT Not at all, not at all. I asked the way. Everyone knows you around here.

THE PROFESSOR I've lived in this town for thirty years. You're new to it, aren't you? How do you like it?

THE STUDENT   I like it fine. It's a pretty town, pleasant. It has a nice park, a boarding school, a bishop, beautiful shops, streets, avenues. . . .

THE PROFESSOR   That's true, Mademoiselle. And yet I wouldn't mind living somewhere else. In Paris or at least Bordeaux.

THE STUDENT   Do you like Bordeaux?

THE PROFESSOR   I don't know. I've never been there.

THE STUDENT   But you know Paris?

THE PROFESSOR   I'm afraid not, Mademoiselle, but if you'll permit me, can you tell me, Paris is the capital of . . . Mademoiselle?

THE STUDENT (*trying to remember, then relieved to get it*)   Paris is the capital of . . . France?

THE PROFESSOR   Yes, Mademoiselle. Bravo! Well done. Perfect. My congratulations. You have your French geography at your fingertips. You know your capitals.

THE STUDENT   Oh! I don't know them all yet, Professor, it's not as easy as that. I have a tough time learning them.

THE PROFESSOR   Oh, it will come. . . . Be brave. . . . Mademoiselle . . . Excuse me . . . You must be patient. . . . Little by little . . . You'll see, it will come. . . . What a nice day . . . well actually, it's not that nice . . . Oh, but it is! What I'm trying to say is it's not nasty, that's the main thing. Uh . . . Uh . . . It's not raining and it's not snowing either.

THE STUDENT   That would be amazing since it's summertime.

THE PROFESSOR   Forgive me, Mademoiselle, I was just going to say . . . but as you'll learn, one must be prepared for anything.

THE STUDENT   So it seems, Professor.

THE PROFESSOR   There's nothing we can be sure of in this world, Mademoiselle.

THE STUDENT   Snow falls in winter. Winter is one of the four seasons. The three others are . . . uh . . . spr . . .

THE PROFESSOR   Yes?

THE STUDENT   Spring and then comes summer . . . and . . . uh . . .

THE PROFESSOR   It sounds like "automobile," Mademoiselle.

THE STUDENT   Ah yes, autumn . . .

THE PROFESSOR   Very good, Mademoiselle. Nicely done, perfect, in fact. I'm convinced you're going to be a good student. You'll make progress, You're intelligent, you seem well-informed with a good memory.

THE STUDENT   Well, I certainly know my seasons, don't I, Professor?

THE PROFESSOR   Yes, indeed, Mademoiselle. Or almost. But it will come. In any case, you're getting there. Soon you'll know all the seasons with your eyes shut. Just like me.

THE STUDENT   It's difficult.

THE PROFESSOR   Not at all. It just takes a little effort and the right attitude, Mademoiselle. You'll see. It will come, rest assured.

THE STUDENT   Oh, I hope so, Professor. I have such a thirst for learning. My parents also want me to broaden my knowledge. They want me to specialize. They think having a grasp of general culture isn't enough these days, no matter how solid it might be.

THE PROFESSOR   Your parents are absolutely right, Mademoiselle. You must pursue your studies. Excuse me for saying so, but it's a necessity. Modern life has become too complex.

THE STUDENT   And too complicated. My parents are well-off, so I'm lucky. They can help me get ahead and pursue my advanced studies.

THE PROFESSOR   And you wish to qualify for . . .

THE STUDENT   The first doctoral exams, as soon as possible. They're in three weeks.

THE PROFESSOR   You already have your baccalaureate, if you don't mind me asking.

THE STUDENT   Yes, Professor. I have a baccalaureate in science and also one in letters.

THE PROFESSOR   Oh, but you're very advanced, perhaps too advanced for your age. And what sort of doctorate do you want to pursue? One in the physical sciences or philosophy?

THE STUDENT   My parents would like me to try for the Total Doctorate, if you think it's possible in such a short time.

THE PROFESSOR   The Total Doctorate? . . . You have a lot of courage, Mademoiselle. I heartily congratulate you. We will try, Mademoiselle, we will try our very best. In any case, you're already quite learned. And for one so young . . .

THE STUDENT   Oh, Professor.

THE PROFESSOR   Now if you'll permit me, if I may . . . I think we should get right to work. We have no time to lose.

THE STUDENT   On the contrary, Professor. That's just what I want. I beg you to begin.

THE PROFESSOR   Then may I ask you to sit down . . . over there. And will you allow me, Mademoiselle, that is if you don't mind, to sit across from you?

THE STUDENT   Certainly, Professor, please do.

THE PROFESSOR   Thank you very much, Mademoiselle.

They sit in profile, facing each other at the table.

THE PROFESSOR   Well, here we are. Do you have your books and notebooks?

THE STUDENT (*taking them out of her briefcase*)   Yes, Professor, of course. I have everything here that I'll need.

THE PROFESSOR   Perfect, Mademoiselle. This is perfect. Then if this won't bore you . . . shall we begin?

THE STUDENT   But of course, Professor. I'm at your disposal, Professor.

THE PROFESSOR   You're at my disposal? (*He gets a sudden gleam in his eye and starts to make a gesture which he quickly suppresses.*) Oh no, Mademoiselle, I'm the one at your disposal. I'm just your humble servant.

THE STUDENT   Oh, Professor . . .

THE PROFESSOR   If you'd like . . . uh . . . we . . . we . . . that is I . . . I could begin by giving you a brief test on your knowledge up to this point, so we can chart your future course. All right then. What are your views on multiplicity?

THE STUDENT   They're a bit vague and confused.

THE PROFESSOR   All right then. Let's give it a whirl.

He rubs his hands together. The Maid enters, which seems to irritate him. She goes to the buffet and takes her time looking for something.

THE PROFESSOR   So, Mademoiselle. How would you like to tackle a little arithmetic, that is, if you're up to it. . . .

THE STUDENT   Oh yes, Professor, certainly. It's my heart's desire.

THE PROFESSOR   It's a rather new science, a modern science, to be exact, more a method than a science. . . . It's also therapeutic. (*to the Maid*) Have you finished, Marie?

THE MAID   Yes, Professor. I found the plate. I'm leaving. . . .

THE PROFESSOR   Then hurry up. Go to your kitchen, please.

THE MAID   Yes, Professor. I'm going. (*starting to leave*) Excuse me, Professor, now pay attention, I beg you to stay calm.

THE PROFESSOR   You're being ridiculous, Marie. Don't worry.

THE MAID   That's what you always say.

THE PROFESSOR   I won't stand for your insinuations. I know perfectly well how to behave. I think I'm old enough.

THE MAID   Exactly, Professor. You'd do better not to start the young lady on arithmetic. Arithmetic tires you out, it's exhausting.

THE PROFESSOR   Not at my age. And why are you butting in? This is my affair. I know what I'm doing. It's none of your business.

THE MAID   All right, Professor. But don't say I didn't warn you.

THE PROFESSOR   I don't need your two cents' worth, Marie.

THE MAID   As you wish, Professor.

She exits.

THE PROFESSOR   Excuse me for that silly interruption, Mademoiselle. Excuse that woman. . . . She's always fretting that I'm going to tire myself out. She worries about my health.

THE STUDENT   All is forgiven, Professor. It just shows she's devoted to you. She loves you very much. Good servants are rare.

THE PROFESSOR   She overreacts. Her fears are stupid. But let's return to our mathematical meanderings.

THE STUDENT   I'm following you, Professor.

THE PROFESSOR (*trying to be funny*)   While remaining seated!

THE STUDENT (*appreciating his joke*)   Just like you, Professor.

THE PROFESSOR   Good. Let's arithmetize a little now.

THE STUDENT   Yes, I can't wait, Professor.

THE PROFESSOR   Would it bore you to tell me . . .

THE STUDENT   Anything, Professor, go on.

THE PROFESSOR   How much are one and one?

THE STUDENT   One and one make two.

THE PROFESSOR (*amazed at her intelligence*)   Oh, that's very good. You seem very advanced in your studies. You'll have no trouble getting your Total Doctorate, Mademoiselle.

THE STUDENT I'm so glad. Particularly hearing it from you.

THE PROFESSOR Moving right along: how much are two and one?

THE STUDENT Three.

THE PROFESSOR Three and one?

THE STUDENT Four.

THE PROFESSOR Four and one?

THE STUDENT Five.

THE PROFESSOR Five and one?

THE STUDENT Six.

THE PROFESSOR Six and one?

THE STUDENT Seven.

THE PROFESSOR Seven and one?

THE STUDENT Eight.

THE PROFESSOR Seven and one?

THE STUDENT Eight . . . *Again.*

THE PROFESSOR Excellent answer! Seven and one?

THE STUDENT Eight. *Once more.*

THE PROFESSOR Perfect. Excellent. Seven and one?

THE STUDENT Eight, *one more time.* And sometimes nine.

THE PROFESSOR Magnificent. You are magnificent You are exquisite. I heartily congratulate you, Mademoiselle. There's no need to continue. You're a master at addition.

Let's try some subtraction. If you're not too exhausted, just tell me how much is four minus three?

THE STUDENT   Four minus three? . . . Four minus three?

THE PROFESSOR   Yes. Or put another way: subtract three from four.

THE STUDENT   That makes . . . seven?

THE PROFESSOR   I'm afraid I have to contradict you, but four minus three is not seven. You're confused: four plus three makes seven, but four minus three doesn't make seven. We're not doing addition anymore, now we're subtracting.

THE STUDENT (*trying to understand*)   Right . . . right . . .

THE PROFESSOR   Four minus three leaves . . . how many? How many?

THE STUDENT   Four?

THE PROFESSOR   No, Mademoiselle, that's not it.

THE STUDENT   Three, then.

THE PROFESSOR   Nor that either, Mademoiselle . . . Pardon me . . . I ought to say . . . it doesn't equal that. . . . Forgive me.

THE STUDENT   Four minus three . . . Four minus three . . . Four minus three? . . . Doesn't that make ten?

THE PROFESSOR   Most certainly not, Mademoiselle. But you shouldn't guess, you should think it through. Let's try to figure it out together. Would you count for me?

THE STUDENT   Yes, Professor. One . . . two . . . uh . . .

THE PROFESSOR   You know how to count, don't you? How far can you count?

THE STUDENT   I can count to . . . infinity.

THE PROFESSOR   But that's impossible, Mademoiselle.

THE STUDENT   Then how about to sixteen?

THE PROFESSOR   That's better. We must know our limits. Please start counting if you will.

THE STUDENT   One . . . two . . . and after two comes three . . . four . . .

THE PROFESSOR   Stop right there, Mademoiselle. Which number is bigger? Three or four?

THE STUDENT   Uh . . . three or four? Which is bigger? The bigger between three or four? In what sense to you mean bigger?

THE PROFESSOR   There are small numbers and big numbers. In big numbers there are more units than in small. . . .

THE STUDENT   Than in small numbers?

THE PROFESSOR   Unless the small ones have smaller units. If they are very small, there might be more units in the smaller numbers than in the big ones . . . that is if it's a matter of other units. . . .

THE STUDENT   In that case, small numbers could be bigger than big numbers?

THE PROFESSOR   Let's not go there. It will take us too far afield. Bear in mind that more than numbers are involved here. There are also magnitudes, sums, groups, there are masses of things, masses—like plums, cars, geese, seeds, etcetera. To make our work easier, let's just suppose we only have equal numbers, then the bigger ones will be those that have the most units.

THE STUDENT   The number with the most is the biggest? Ah, I understand, Professor, you're equating quality with quantity.

THE PROFESSOR   That's too theoretical, Mademoiselle, much too theoretical. Don't worry about that. Let's take an example and figure it out with a specific case. We'll leave sweeping conclusions for later. All right, we have the number four and the number three, each always has the same number of units; which number will be bigger, the smaller one or the bigger one?

THE STUDENT   Excuse me, Professor. . . . What do you mean by the bigger number? Is that the one that isn't as small as the other?

THE PROFESSOR   That's right, Mademoiselle. Perfect. You've understood me perfectly.

THE STUDENT   Then it's four.

THE PROFESSOR   What is this four? Is it bigger or smaller than three?

THE STUDENT   Smaller . . . no, bigger.

THE PROFESSOR   Excellent answer! How many units are there between three and four? Or between four and three, if you prefer?

THE STUDENT   There are no units between three and four, Professor. Four comes right after three; so there's nothing between three and four!

THE PROFESSOR   I haven't made myself understood. It's obviously my fault. I wasn't clear enough,

THE STUDENT   No, Professor, it's my fault.

THE PROFESSOR   Hold on. . . . Here are three matches. And here's another, that makes four. Now watch carefully. . . . We have four and I take away one, how many are left?

The audience can't see these matches or any of the other objects he mentions. The Professor rises from the table and writes on an imaginary blackboard with an imaginary piece of chalk, etc.

THE STUDENT   Five. If three and one make four, then four and one make five.

THE PROFESSOR   That's not it. That's not it at all. You have a tendency to keep adding. But one must also subtract. You can't just integrate, you also have to disintegrate. That's how life is. With philosophy. With science. It's what we call progress, civilization.

THE STUDENT   Yes, Professor.

THE PROFESSOR   Let's return to our matches. I have four of them. You see there are exactly four. I take one away and how many are left. . . .

THE STUDENT   I don't know, Professor.

THE PROFESSOR   Come on, think. It's not easy, I admit, but you're smart enough to handle the intellectual challenge required to understand. So then . . .

THE STUDENT   I don't get it, Professor. I just don't know, Professor.

THE PROFESSOR   Then let's try a simpler example. If you had two noses and I pulled one of them off, how many would you have left?

THE STUDENT   None.

THE PROFESSOR   How do you get none?

THE STUDENT   Because you haven't pulled any off, I still have one. If you'd pulled it off, it would be gone.

THE PROFESSOR   You haven't understood my example. Suppose you have only one ear.

THE STUDENT   Yes, and then?

THE PROFESSOR   I add another. How many would you have then?

THE STUDENT   Two.

THE PROFESSOR   Good. And I add one more. Then how many would you have?

THE STUDENT   Three ears.

THE PROFESSOR   I take one away . . . how many ears remain?

THE STUDENT   Two.

THE PROFESSOR   Good. I take away another one. How many are left?

THE STUDENT   Two.

THE PROFESSOR   No. You have two, I take one, I eat it, how many are left?

THE STUDENT   Two.

THE PROFESSOR   I eat one of them. One.

THE STUDENT   Two.

THE PROFESSOR   One.

THE STUDENT Two.

THE PROFESSOR One!

THE STUDENT Two!

THE PROFESSOR One!!

THE STUDENT Two!!

THE PROFESSOR One!!!

THE STUDENT Two!!!

THE PROFESSOR One!!!!

THE STUDENT Two!!!!

THE PROFESSOR No, no, that's not right. The example isn't . . . it's a poor example. . . . Now pay attention.

THE STUDENT Yes, professor.

THE PROFESSOR You have . . . you have . . . you have . . .

THE STUDENT Ten fingers!

THE PROFESSOR If you like. Perfect. Good. You have ten fingers.

THE STUDENT Yes, Professor.

THE PROFESSOR How many would you have if you had five?

THE STUDENT Ten, Professor.

THE PROFESSOR That's not right!

THE STUDENT Yes, Professor.

THE PROFESSOR I said no!

THE STUDENT You just told me I had ten. . . .

THE PROFESSOR   But then I said you had five right after that!

THE STUDENT   But I don't have five, I have ten!

THE PROFESSOR   Let's try something else. . . . For the purpose of subtraction, let's limit ourselves to numbers between one and five. Just wait, Mademoiselle, you'll see. I'll help you understand.

He begins to write on the imaginary blackboard. He moves it closer to her and she turns to look at it.

THE PROFESSOR   Now watch, Mademoiselle.

He pretends to draw a stick on the blackboard and writes the number "1" underneath it. Then he draws two sticks with the number "2" underneath that, then three sticks with the number "3" underneath that and finally four sticks with the number "4" beneath that.

THE PROFESSOR   You see.

THE STUDENT   Yes, Professor.

THE PROFESSOR   These are sticks, Mademoiselle, sticks. This is one stick, there are two sticks, three sticks, four sticks and then five sticks. One stick, two sticks, three sticks, four and five sticks, these are the numbers. When we count sticks, each stick is a unit, Mademoiselle. What did I just say?

THE STUDENT   "A unit, Mademoiselle. What did I just say?"

THE PROFESSOR   Or a figure, or a number. One, two, three, four, five, these are the elements of numeration, Mademoiselle.

THE STUDENT (*unsure*)   Yes, Professor. The elements, the figures which are sticks, the units and numbers . . .

THE PROFESSOR   At the same time . . . That is to say, in sum, arithmetic herself steps forth in all her glory.

THE STUDENT   Yes, Professor. Very good, Professor. Thank you, Professor.

THE PROFESSOR   All right now, count if you will while using these elements. . . . Add and subtract . . .

THE STUDENT (*struggling to burn them into her memory*)   Sticks are really figures and numbers are units?

THE PROFESSOR   Hmmmm. In a manner of speaking. And then?

THE STUDENT   One can subtract two units from three units, but can one subtract two twos from three threes? And two figures from four numbers? And three numbers from one unit?

THE PROFESSOR   No, Mademoiselle.

THE STUDENT   Why not, Professor?

THE PROFESSOR   Because, Mademoiselle.

THE STUDENT   Because why, Professor? Because one is the same as the other?

THE PROFESSOR   That's just the way it is, Mademoiselle. It can't be explained. It comes through internal mathematical reasoning. You either have it or you don't.

THE STUDENT   Just my luck!

THE PROFESSOR   Listen, Mademoiselle, if you're unable to understand these principles, these mathematical archetypes, you'll never be able to do the proper work of an engineer and will be even more at sea trying to teach at a polytechnical school, to say nothing of an advanced nursery school. I realize this isn't easy, it's very, very abstract . . . obviously. . . . But how do you expect to be able to solve problems in your head, unless you understand the basic elements, which is the least an ordinary engineer can do — how much for example is three billion, seven hundred fifty-five million, nine hundred ninety-eight thousand, two hundred and fifty-one, multiplied by five billion, one hundred sixty-two million, three hundred and three thousand, five hundred and eight?

THE STUDENT (*with the speed of light*)   Nineteen quintillion, three hundred ninety quadrillion, two trillion, eight hundred and forty-four billion, two hundred and nineteen million, one hundred and sixty-four thousand, five hundred and eight . . .

THE PROFESSOR (*astonished*)   No. I don't think so. It should come to nineteen quintillion, three hundred ninety quadrillion, two trillion, eight hundred and forty-four billion, two hundred and nineteen million, one hundred sixty-four thousand, five hundred and nine . . .

THE STUDENT   No . . . five hundred and eight . . .

THE PROFESSOR (*increasingly astonished, calculating mentally*) Yes . . . You're right . . . the total is indeed . . . (*muttering incoherently*) . . . quintillions, quadrillions, trillions, billions, millions . . . (*clear as a bell*) one hundred sixty-four thousand five hundred and eight . . . (*stupefied*) But how did you figure it out if you can't grasp the principles of arithmetical reasoning?

THE STUDENT   Easy. Since I don't trust my ability to think things through, I just memorized all the possible sums of all the possible numbers that could be multiplied.

THE PROFESSOR   Very impressive. But I have to confess I'm not satisfied. I can't congratulate you, Mademoiselle: in mathematics, particularly in arithmetic, what counts most (because arithmetic depends on counting) is understanding. You can count on it. It's through mathematical reasoning, simultaneously inductive and deductive, that you'll find the answer, as well as any other answer. Mathematics is the sworn enemy of memory, which is excellent in and of itself, but dangerous arithmetically speaking! So I'm not pleased. . . . This won't do . . . no, it won't do at all. . . .

THE STUDENT (*crushed*)   No, Professor.

THE PROFESSOR   Let's drop it for now and move on to something else.

THE STUDENT   Yes, Professor.

THE MAID (*entering*)   Um, um . . . Professor . . .

THE PROFESSOR (*not hearing her*)   It's a pity, Mademoiselle, that you're so far behind in advanced mathematics.

THE MAID (*pulling his sleeve*)   Professor! Professor!

THE PROFESSOR   I'm afraid you won't qualify for a Total Doctorate. . . .

THE STUDENT   Yes, Professor, what a shame!

THE PROFESSOR   Unless of course . . . (*to The Maid*) Leave me alone, Marie. See here, why are you butting in? Go back to your kitchen! Back to your pots and pans! Go! Vamoose! (*to The Student*) We'll try to prepare you for a partial doctorate, at least. . . .

THE MAID   Professor! Professor! (*pulling on his sleeve again*)

THE PROFESSOR (*to The Maid*)   Take your hands off me! I said, hands off! What is the meaning of this? (*to The Student*) Look, if you want to pursue a partial doctorate, I'll try and teach you . . .

THE STUDENT   Yes, Professor.

THE PROFESSOR   . . . the elements of linguistics and comparative philology.

THE MAID   No, Professor, no! You mustn't!

THE PROFESSOR   Marie, you're overreacting!

THE MAID   Anything but philology, Professor, philology leads to disaster. . . .

THE STUDENT (*astonished*)   To disaster? (*smiling stupidly*) That's a good one!

THE PROFESSOR (*to The Maid*)   You're going overboard. Get out!

THE MAID   All right, Professor, all right. But you can't say I didn't warn you. Philology leads to disaster.

THE PROFESSOR   I'm a grown man, Marie!

THE STUDENT   Yes, Professor.

THE MAID   As you wish. (*She exits.*)

THE PROFESSOR   Let's press on, Mademoiselle.

THE STUDENT   Yes, Professor.

THE PROFESSOR   Now please give your undivided attention to this lecture I've prepared. . . .

THE STUDENT   Yes, Professor.

THE PROFESSOR   Thanks to which, in fifteen short minutes you'll be able to aquire the fundamental principles of linguistic and comparative philology of neo-Spanish languages.

THE STUDENT   Oh yes, Professor, yes! (*clapping her hands*)

THE PROFESSOR (*sternly*)   Silence! What's the meaning of this?

THE STUDENT   Forgive me, Professor. (*She slowly puts her hands back on the table.*)

THE PROFESSOR   Silence!

He rises and paces around the room with his hands behind his back, stopping from time to time center stage or near the Student, punctuating his words with gestures; he holds forth without overdoing it. The Student struggles to keep her eyes on him, but has a hard time following him since she has to keep turning her head. One or two times she has to make a complete turn.

THE PROFESSOR   All right then, Mademoiselle . . . Spanish is the mother tongue from which all neo-Spanish languages derive: to wit, Spanish, Latin, Italian, our own French, Portuguese, Rumanian, Sardinian, or Sardiniapalian, Spanish and neo-Spanish. It also enjoys close ties to Turkish, for obvious reasons. Turkish is akin to Greek, which is only logical since Turkey is a neighbor of Greece which is even closer to Turkey than I am to you. This further illustrates an important law of linguistics, namely that geography and philology are twin sisters. Feel free to take notes, Mademoiselle.

THE STUDENT (*in a lifeless voice*)   Yes, Professor.

THE PROFESSOR   What distinguishes the neo-Spanish tongues and idioms from each other and from the other linguistic groups, to wit: the Austrian and neo-Austrian or Hapsburgian, as well as the group that includes Esperanto, Helvetia, Monegasque, Swiss, Andorran, Basque and jai alai, to say nothing of the diplomatic and technical language groups—what distinguishes them, I repeat, is their striking similarity, which makes it so hard to tell them apart. I'm speaking of course of the neo-Spanish languages which can only be discerned by their distinct characteristics, thereby offering indisputable proof of their remarkable resemblance, rendering their common origin indisputable, which makes them profoundly different because of the ongoing similarities I just mentioned.

THE STUDENT Ohhhh! Yesssss, Professor!

THE PROFESSOR But let's not dwell on generalities. . . .

THE STUDENT (*disappointed but resigned*) Oh, Professor . . .

THE PROFESSOR This seems to intrigue you. That's a good sign, a very good sign.

THE STUDENT Oh, yes, Professor . . .

THE PROFESSOR Don't worry, Mademoiselle. We'll come back to it later . . . to the extent one can ever go back. Who's to say?

THE STUDENT (*enchanted, in spite of everything*) Oh, yes, Professor

THE PROFESSOR Every tongue, Mademoiselle . . . Now pay attention, you must remember this *till the very hour of your death.* . . .

THE STUDENT Oh! yes, Professor, *till the very hour of my death* . . . Yes, Professor . . .

THE PROFESSOR . . . and again this is another basic principle —every tongue, in essence, is nothing but language, implying of course that it's made up of sounds, or . . .

THE STUDENT Phonemes . . .

THE PROFESSOR You snatched the words right out of my mouth. Don't flaunt your knowledge. You should listen instead.

THE STUDENT Very good, Professor. Yes, Professor.

THE PROFESSOR Sounds, Mademoiselle, must be plucked by their wings as they become airborne, so they don't fall on deaf ears. It follows that when you're ready to enunciate you should make every effort to lift your chin and neck as high as possible and rise up on your tiptoes, this way you'll—

THE STUDENT Yes, Professor.

THE PROFESSOR Button your lip! Stay seated and don't interrupt. . . . And project the sounds loud and clear, using all your lung power in tandem with your vocal cords. Like this: watch me: "Butterfly," "Eureka," "Trafalgar," "Papaya," "Popageno." This way the sounds swell with warm air, enabling them to float aloft and rise without risk of falling on deaf dears, which are veritable voids, tombs of tremulous tones. If you utter several sounds rapidly, they will automatically cling to each other, forming syllables, words, even sentences, that is to say, swarms of seething significance, innately irrational assemblages of sound drained of all sense, and for that very reason, capable of rising to dizzy altitudes without risk. Left to their own devices, these high-flying words will collapse, weighted down by their significance. They always deflate at the end, tumbling down . . .

THE STUDENT . . . onto deaf ears.

THE PROFESSOR That's right, but don't interrupt. . . . disintegrating into gibberish. Or else they burst like balloons. Therefore, Mademoiselle . . .

The Student suddenly seems to be in pain.

THE PROFESSOR What's wrong?

THE STUDENT I have a toothache, Professor.

THE PROFESSOR So what? We're not going to stop for such a piddling detail. On we go . . .

THE STUDENT (*whose pain is escalating*) Yes, Professor.

THE PROFESSOR Let me direct your attention to the consonants whose nature changes in combinations. F's become v's, d's become t's, and g's become k's and vice versa as in the examples I'm about to give you: "three o'clock, the children, chicken cutlets, modern times, night must fall."

THE STUDENT I have a toothache.

THE PROFESSOR On we go.

THE STUDENT Yes.

THE PROFESSOR As I was saying . . . It takes years and years to learn how to pronounce correctly. Thanks to science, we can do it in a matter of minutes. To project words, sounds or whatever else you fancy, you must brazenly expel the air from your lungs and then let it float over the vocal cords with the utmost delicacy, caressing them ever so slightly—like harps or leaves swirling in the wind—until they start to tremble, shudder and vibrate, vibrate, vibrate or uvulate or pulsate, rubbing against each other—gyrating, gyrating, everything moving: the uvula, tongue, palate, teeth . . .

THE STUDENT I have a toothache.

THE PROFESSOR   . . . lips. . . . Finally the words flow out the nose, the mouth, the ears, the pores, carrying all the body parts we've mentioned along with them, torn up by the roots in a symphonic spasm which we incorrectly label the voice—whether subdued in song or transformed to an atonal typhoon with all the trappings—wreaths of fabulous flowers and sonorous sibilants—labials, dentals, occlusives, palatals and others—some caressing and others toxic or terrifying. . . .

THE STUDENT   Yes, Professor, I have a toothache.

THE PROFESSOR   Onward, onward. Neo-Spanish languages are so intimately related to each other that they can be mistaken for actual second cousins. They share the same mother—Spanish with a silent e. That's why it's so hard to tell them apart. And why it's so important to articulate well to avoid errors of pronunciation. Pronunciation is a language unto itself. Bad pronunciation can get you in hot water. Since we're on the subject, let me share (parenthetically, of course) a personal memory with you.

A pause. The Professor briefly gets lost in his past. His features soften, but he quickly pulls himself together.

THE PROFESSOR   I was very young, almost a child. I was doing my military service. I had a friend in my regiment, a viscount, who had a serious speech defect: he couldn't pronounce the letter f. Instead of f, he said f. Thus, instead of saying, "Familiarity breeds contempt," he said, "Familiarity breeds contempt." He said "feminine" instead of "feminine"; "Frescobaldi" instead of "Frescobaldi"; "french fry" instead of "french fry"; "fuck off" instead of "fuck off"; "fandango" instead of "fandango"; "fee-fi-fo-fum" instead of "fee-fi-fo-fum"; "Philippe" instead of "Philippe"; "fictory" instead of "fictory"; "February" instead of "February"; "March-April" instead of "March-April"; "Frère Jacques", mis-pronounced "Frère Jacques"; "Mont Blanc" instead of "Mont Blanc," etcetera; "etcetera" instead of "etcetera," and "thus and so on" instead of "etcetera"; etcetera and so on. Thanks to his hats, however, he was able to hide this defect, so no one ever noticed it.

THE STUDENT Yes. I have a toothache.

THE PROFESSOR (*suddenly turning harsh*) Onward and upward! Let's start with the similarities between these languages, so we can better understand their differences later on. These differences are barely perceptible to those who aren't aware of them. Thus, all the words of all these languages . . .

THE STUDENT Ah yes . . . ? I have a toothache.

THE PROFESSOR On we go . . . are always the same, just as all the endings, prefixes, suffixes and roots . . .

THE STUDENT Are the roots of words square?

THE PROFESSOR Square or cubed. It depends.

THE STUDENT I have a toothache.

THE PROFESSOR On we go. Thus, to give you an example, which is merely an illustration, take the word "front." . . .

THE STUDENT Where should I take it?

THE PROFESSOR Wherever you want as long as you take it, but don't interrupt.

THE STUDENT I have a toothache.

THE PROFESSOR On we go . . . I said, Onward and upward! Now take the French word "front." Have you taken it?

THE STUDENT Yes, yes, I've got it. My teeth, my teeth . . .

THE PROFESSOR The word "front" is the root of "frontispiece" and also of "affronted." "Ispice" is the suffix and "af" the prefix. They're labeled like this because they don't change. They don't want to.

THE STUDENT I have a toothache.

THE PROFESSOR On we go. Quickly now. These prefixes are Spanish in origin. I trust you noticed. You did, didn't you?

THE STUDENT Oh! How my tooth aches!

THE PROFESSOR Onward and upward. You should also have noticed that they haven't changed in French. So, Mademoiselle, nothing can change them, not Latin, not Italian, not Portuguese, not Sardanapalian, or Sardanapali, not Rumanian, not Neo-Spanish, not Spanish nor even the Asian influence: "front," "frontispiece," "affronted" are always the same word with the same root. They share the same suffix and prefix in every language I've mentioned. And it's ever thus with every word.

THE STUDENT These words say the same thing in every language? I have a toothache.

THE PROFESSOR Absolutely. How could it be otherwise? They always have the same meaning, the same makeup and the same sonorous structure. I'm not only talking about this particular word, but every conceivable word in every language, because ideas are expressed by one and the same word in all countries and that goes for their synonyms too. Forget about your teeth.

THE STUDENT   My teeth hurt. Yes, yes and yes.

THE PROFESSOR   Good, on we go. I said, on we go. For example, how would you say in French: My grandmother's roses are as yellow as my Asian grandfather.

THE STUDENT   My teeth ache, ache, ache.

THE PROFESSOR   Keep going, keep going, answer me just the same!

THE STUDENT   In French?

THE PROFESSOR   In French.

THE STUDENT   Uh . . . I should say in French: My grandmother's roses are . . . ?

THE PROFESSOR   As yellow as my Asian grandfather . . .

THE STUDENT   All right. I think the French goes: The roses of my . . . How do you say grandmother in French?

THE PROFESSOR   In French? Grandmother.

THE STUDENT   My grandmother's roses are as . . . yellow . . . In French you say, yellow, right?

THE PROFESSOR   Yes, of course.

THE STUDENT   Are as yellow as my grandfather when he's angry.

THE PROFESSOR   No. Your grandfather who's A . . .

THE STUDENT   Sian . . . I have a toothache.

THE PROFESSOR   That's it.

THE STUDENT   I have a tooth . . .

THE PROFESSOR   Ache . . . too bad . . . Onward and upward! Now translate the same sentence in Spanish and then neo-Spanish.

THE STUDENT   In Spanish that would be: My grandmother's roses are as yellow as my Asian grandfather.

THE PROFESSOR   No, that's wrong.

THE STUDENT   And in neo-Spanish: My grandmother's roses are as yellow as my Asian grandfather.

THE PROFESSOR   Wrong, wrong, wrong! You've inverted the two. You've taken Spanish for neo-Spanish and neo-Spanish for Spanish. . . . Oh . . . no . . . it's the other way around. . . .

THE STUDENT   I have a toothache. You're getting mixed up.

THE PROFESSOR   And you're the one who's mixing me up. Pay attention and take notes. I'll say it in Spanish, then neo-Spanish and finally in Latin. You will repeat after me. Take care because the resemblances are huge. In fact they're identical. Now listen and follow carefully. . . .

THE STUDENT   I have a tooth . . .

THE PROFESSOR   Ache.

THE STUDENT   Onward and upward . . . Ah!

THE PROFESSOR   In Spanish: My grandmother's roses are as yellow as my Asian grandfather; in Latin: My grandmother's roses are as yellow as my Asian grandfather. Can you detect the differences? Now translate it into . . . Rumanian.

THE STUDENT   How do you say roses in Rumanian?

THE PROFESSOR   Roses. What else?

THE STUDENT   But it's not roses. Oh, I have such a toothache. . . .

THE PROFESSOR   No, no, certainly not, since roses is the Asian translation of the word roses in English, Spanish and Sardanapalian. Do you understand?

THE STUDENT   Excuse me, Professor, but . . . Oh what a toothache . . . I don't see the difference.

THE PROFESSOR   But it's so simple! So very simple! It's just a matter of experience, having technical experience and practice with these diverse languages, which remain diverse in spite of their sharing so many identical characteristics. I'm going to try and give you the key. . . .

THE STUDENT   Toothache.

THE PROFESSOR   What differentiates these languages is neither the words, which are always the same, nor the sentence structure, which is also the same, nor the intonation, which offers no differences, nor the rhythms. . . . What differentiates them . . . Are you listening?

THE STUDENT   I have a toothache.

THE PROFESSOR   Are you listening to me, Mademoiselle? Aah! We're going to lose our temper.

THE STUDENT   You're driving me crazy, Professor. I have a toothache.

THE PROFESSOR   I don't give a flying fuck! Listen to me!

THE STUDENT   All right . . . yes . . . yes . . . go on. . . .

THE PROFESSOR   What distinguishes them from each other and from their mother Spanish with its silent e is . . .

THE STUDENT (*wincing*)   Is what?

THE PROFESSOR   Ineffable. Something ineffable you can only detect after Herculean effort and grueling experience.

THE STUDENT   Ah?

THE PROFESSOR   Yes, Mademoiselle. No one can hand you these rules. It takes intuition, that's all there is to it. And to get it you have to study, study and then study some more.

THE STUDENT   Toothache.

THE PROFESSOR   All the same, there are a few specific cases in which words differ from one language to another . . . but we can't rely on them because, in a manner of speaking, they're exceptional.

THE STUDENT   Ah, yes? Oh Professor, I have a toothache.

THE PROFESSOR   Don't interrupt! Don't make me lose my temper! I can't answer for what I might do. As I was saying . . . Ah yes, these exceptional cases, that is to say the ones that are clearly distinguishable, or distinguishable enough . . . that is to say, readily distinguishable if you prefer . . . I repeat: If you prefer, because I can't help noticing that you're not listening to me. . . .

THE STUDENT   I have a toothache.

THE PROFESSOR   As I was saying: in certain expressions that are currently in use, certain words totally differ from one language to another, so much so that the language being spoken is much easier to identify. I'll give you an example: the neo-Spanish expression favored in Madrid: "My country is neo-Spain" in Italian becomes, "My country is . . ."

THE STUDENT   Neo-Spain!

THE PROFESSOR   No! "My country is Italy." Now tell me, via simple deduction, how do you say Italy in French?

THE STUDENT   I have a toothache!

THE PROFESSOR   But it's so simple: for the word Italy, we have the French word France, which is an exact translation. My country is France. And France in Asian becomes Asia! My country is Asia. And Asia in Portuguese becomes Portugal! The Asian expression My country is Asia is translated the very same way into Portuguese: My country is Portugal! And so on.

THE STUDENT   Enough! Enough! My teeth . . .

THE PROFESSOR   Ache! Your teeth, your teeth, your teeth! . . . Keep it up and I'm going to pull them out myself! Now here's another example. The word capital takes on different meanings depending on the language you're speaking. If a Spaniard says, I live in the capital, the word capital doesn't refer to the same place that a Portuguese has in mind when he says, I live in the capital. This is even truer for a Frenchman, a neo-Spaniard, a Rumanian, a Latin and a Sardanapalian. . . . Whenever you hear it, Mademoiselle . . . Mademoiselle, I'm talking to you, for Christ's sake! Whenever you hear the expression I live in the capital, you'll immediately know whether it's Spanish or Spanish, or neo-Spanish, or French, or Asian, or Rumanian, or Latin according to how the phrase is pronounced. You'll be able to tell which city's being referred to the moment it's uttered. But alas, these are the only concrete examples I can give you. . . .

THE STUDENT   Oh, oh, oh . . . my teeth!

THE PROFESSOR   Silence! Or I'll bash your head in!

THE STUDENT   Go ahead and try! Pompous asshole!

The Professor grabs her wrist and twists it hard.

THE STUDENT   Ow!

THE PROFESSOR   Easy does it! Shut your trap!

THE STUDENT (*whimpering*)   Tooth ache . . .

THE PROFESSOR   The dilemma here . . . how should I put it?
. . . The most paradoxical . . . yes . . . that's the word . . .
the most paradoxical aspect of the dilemma is that people
who are completely uneducated can speak these different
languages. . . . Did you hear that? What did I just say?

THE STUDENT   . . . can speak these different languages! What
did I just say?

THE PROFESSOR   You were lucky this time! Many people
speak Spanish chock full of neo-Spanish words they're not
even aware of, thinking they're speaking Latin. . . . Or they
speak Latin, chock full of Asian words, thinking they're
speaking Rumanian. . . . Or Spanish, chock full of neo-
Spanish, thinking they're speaking Sardanapali, or Spanish
. . . Do you understand?

THE STUDENT   Yes! Yes! Yes! Yes! What do you want from
me?

THE PROFESSOR   Mind your manners, honey bunch, or
you'll be sorry. (*in a rage*) To crown it all off, Mademoiselle,
certain people say, "My two livers bother me since I'm a high
liver" in Latin, thinking they're speaking Spanish to a
Frenchman who doesn't understand a word of Spanish; yet
he understands it as if it were his own language. In fact, he
thinks it is his own language. And this Frenchman will reply

in French, "Me too, Monsieur, my two livers bother me," which will be perfectly understood by a Spaniard, who'll think he's speaking pure Spanish, that they're both speaking Spanish, when in fact it's neither Spanish, nor French, but Latin in the neo-Spanish manner. . . . Sit still, Mademoiselle . . . stop wiggling your legs and don't tap your feet. . . .

THE STUDENT   I have a toothache.

THE PROFESSOR   How does the man in the street communicate with anyone when he doesn't know what language he's speaking while operating under the false assumption it's the right one?

THE STUDENT   That's what I'd like to know.

THE PROFESSOR   It's just one of those unaccountable mysteries embedded in his genes—not to be confused with experience—it's a paradox, an anomaly, a quirk of human nature, in a word, it's instinct pure and simple—and that's all there is to it.

THE STUDENT   Ha! Ha!

THE PROFESSOR   Instead of gazing at the flies on the wall while I'm out here busting my ass, you'd do better to try and pay attention. . . . I'm not the one going up for my partial doctorate . . . I got it a long time ago . . . I completed my Total Doctorate . . . as well as my Super-Total Doctorate. . . . Don't you realize I'm just looking after your own good?

THE STUDENT   Tooth ache!

THE PROFESSOR   Spoiled brat . . . I can't take it anymore, can't take it anymore, can't take it anymore, can't take it anymore. . . .

THE STUDENT   I'm . . . listening. . . . I'm . . . listening. . . .

THE PROFESSOR   Ah! To reiterate: if you want to tell these different languages apart, nothing succeeds like practice. Let's tackle them in order. I'll begin with all the translations of the word dagger.

THE STUDENT   Whatever you say. After all . . .

THE PROFESSOR   (*calling her*)   Marie! Marie! She isn't coming. . . . Marie! Marie . . . See here, Marie. (*Opening the door to the right*) Marie! . . .

He exits. The Student is alone several moments. She stares into space, blankly.

THE PROFESSOR   (*offstage, in a shrill voice*)   Marie! What's going on? Why aren't you coming? When I ask you to come, you come!

He enters, followed by Marie.

THE PROFESSOR   I give the orders, do you hear me? (*pointing to the Student*) She doesn't understand a thing, that girl! She just doesn't get it.

THE MAID   Don't rile yourself up, Professor. You know what happens. You're going to go too far, way too far.

THE PROFESSOR   I know how to stop myself in time.

THE MAID   That's what you always say. I'd like to see it.

THE STUDENT   I have a toothache.

THE MAID   You see, it's starting, that's the symptom!

THE PROFESSOR   What symptom? What do you mean? What are you trying to say?

THE STUDENT (*weakly*)   Yes, what are you trying to say? I have a toothache.

THE MAID   The final symptom! The penultimate symptom!

THE PROFESSOR   Bullshit! Bullshit! Bullshit!

The Maid starts to exit.

THE PROFESSOR   Don't walk out on me! I called you to help me look for my daggers from Spain, neo-Spain, Portugal, France, Asia, Rumania, Sardanapali, the Latin countries and Spain.

THE MAID (*severely*)   Don't count on me. (*She exits.*)

The Professor starts to protest, but restrains himself, at a loss. Then he suddenly remembers.

THE PROFESSOR   Ah!

He hurries to the desk drawer, where he finds a large invisible dagger, which could also be real, depending on the director's taste. He grabs it and waves it gleefully.

THE PROFESSOR   Here's one, Mademoiselle. Here's a dagger. It's a pity we only have this one, but we'll try to make it do for all the languages! All you have to do is pronounce the word dagger in every language, look at it long and hard and then picture it in the language you're speaking.

THE STUDENT   I have a toothache.

THE PROFESSOR (*singing, almost chanting*)   Now say *dag*, like *dag, ger* . . . Look at it, look at it, look at it long and hard . . .

THE STUDENT   And which one is it? French? Italian or Spanish?

THE PROFESSOR   It doesn't matter anymore. It doesn't affect you. Say: *dag*.

THE STUDENT   *Dag*.

THE PROFESSOR   . . . *ger*. Look at it. (*waving it under her eyes*)

THE STUDENT   *Ger* . . .

THE PROFESSOR   Again . . . Look at it.

THE STUDENT   No! Goddammit! I've had enough! And besides, my teeth hurt, my feet hurt, and my head hurts . . .

THE PROFESSOR   (*in a staccato voice*)   *Dagger* . . . look at it . . . *dagger* . . . look at it . . . *dagger* . . . look at it. . . .

THE STUDENT   You're giving me an earache too. Oh, that voice! It's so shrill!

THE PROFESSOR   Say: *dagger* . . . *dag* . . . *ger* . . .

THE STUDENT   No! I have an earache. I ache everywhere . . .

THE PROFESSOR   I'm going to rip them off, that's what I'm going to do! . . . Damn ears! Then they won't hurt anymore, my sweet!

THE STUDENT   Ah . . . but you're the one who's hurting me. . . .

THE PROFESSOR   Look at it. Come on, hurry up, repeat after me: *dag* . . .

THE STUDENT   All right, if you insist . . . *dag* . . . *dagger* . . . (*in a moment of ironic lucidity*) Is that neo-Spanish . . .

THE PROFESSOR If you like, yes, it's neo–Spanish, but hurry up . . . we don't have much time. . . . And what did you mean by that stupid question? What are you up to?

THE STUDENT (*becoming increasingly exhausted, weeping and desperate, but at the same time riled up, in a sort of ecstasy*) Ah!

THE PROFESSOR Repeat after me, look at it. (*imitating a cuckoo*) Dagger . . . dagger . . . dagger . . . dagger . . .

THE STUDENT Ohhh . . . I have such an ache . . . my head . . . (*naming the parts of her body as she gently caresses them with her hand*) . . . my eyes . . .

THE PROFESSOR (*still like a cuckoo*) Dagger . . . dagger . . .

They're both standing. The Professor keeps waving his invisible dagger, almost beside himself, as he circles her in a sort of scalp dance. These steps shouldn't be exaggerated, just suggested. The Student stands facing the audience, then retreats toward the window, sluggish and ill, as if in a trance.

THE PROFESSOR Repeat after me, repeat after me: *dagger . . . dagger . . . dagger . . .*

THE STUDENT Everything aches . . . my throat . . . *dag* . . . my neck . . . oh, my shoulders, my breasts . . . *dagger* . . .

THE PROFESSOR *Dagger . . . dagger . . . dagger . . .*

THE STUDENT My hips . . . *dagger* . . . my thighs . . . *dag* . . .

THE PROFESSOR Mind your pronunciation . . . *dagger* . . . *dagger* . . .

THE STUDENT *Dagger* . . . my throat . . .

THE PROFESSOR *Dagger . . . dagger . . .*

THE STUDENT *Dagger . . .* my shoulders, my arms, my breasts, my hips . . . *dagger . . . dagger . . .*

THE PROFESSOR That's it. Now you're pronouncing well. . . .

THE STUDENT *Dagger . . .* my breasts . . . my belly . . .

THE PROFESSOR (*changing his voice*) Watch out . . . don't break my windows . . . the dagger kills. . . .

THE STUDENT (*in a weak voice*) Yes, yes . . . the dagger kills?

THE PROFESSOR (*killing her with a spectacular thrust of the dagger*) Aaah! So be it!

Murderer and victim cry "Aaah!" simultaneously. The Student then falls into a chair near the window, landing in an obscene position, her legs spread wide on either side of the chair. The Professor stands over her with his back to the audience and plunges the dagger in a second time, slashing her upward, from bottom to top, his entire body convulsing in a prolonged shudder

THE PROFESSOR (*winded, mumbling*) Bitch . . . That was good. . . . That did me good. . . . Ah! . . . Ah! . . . I'm wiped out. I can hardly breathe. . . . Aaaah!

He struggles for breath and falls; luckily a chair is there; he mops his brow, muttering incomprehensibly; his breathing returns to normal. . . . He rises and looks at the dagger in his hand, he gazes at the young girl and is suddenly stricken with panic, as if waking from a dream.

THE PROFESSOR What have I done? What's going to happen to me now? What's going to happen? Son of a . . . This is not good, not good at all! Mademoiselle? Mademoiselle, get up! (*agitated, not knowing what to do with the invisible dagger in his hand*) See here, young lady, the lesson is over. . . . You may go. . . . You can pay me another time. . . . Oh! she's dead . . . dead, dead. . . . And by my dagger . . . She is dead. . . . This is terrible. (*calling the maid*) Marie! Marie! My dear Marie, come here! Oh! Oh! (*The door to the right opens. Marie appears.*) No . . . don't come in. . . . I made a mistake. . . . I don't need you, Marie. . . . I don't need you anymore . . . do you hear me? . . .

Marie enters looking stern, she eyes the corpse without saying a word.

THE PROFESSOR (*increasingly undone*)   I don't need you, Marie. . . .

THE MAID (*sarcastic*)   So, are you pleased with your student, did she do well with her lesson?

THE PROFESSOR (*hiding the dagger behind his back*)   Yes, the lesson is finished . . . but . . . she . . . she's still here . . . she doesn't want to leave.

THE MAID (*harshly*)   So it seems!

THE PROFESSOR (*trembling*)   I didn't do it. . . . It wasn't me. . . . Marie . . . No . . . I swear . . . I didn't do it, my little Marie. . . .

THE MAID   Then who was it? Who did this? Me?

THE PROFESSOR   I don't know. . . . Maybe . . .

THE MAID   Or the cat?

THE PROFESSOR   It's possible. I don't know. . . .

THE MAID   This is the fortieth time today! . . . Every day it's the same thing! Every day! You should be ashamed of yourself . . . at your age. . . . You're going to make yourself sick! You won't have any more students. It will serve you right.

THE PROFESSOR (*angry*)   It's not my fault. She didn't want to learn! She was defiant. She was a bad student! She didn't want to learn!

THE MAID   Liar!

THE PROFESSOR (*slyly approaching her with the dagger behind his back*)   It's none of your business!

The Professor tries to give her a serious blow with the dagger, but the Maid seizes his wrist and twists it hard. The Professor drops his weapon.

THE PROFESSOR   I'm sorry!

The Maid slaps him with two resounding blows. The Professor falls to the floor on his ass, sniveling.

THE MAID   Little murderer! Bastard! Filthy pig! You were going to try that on me? I'm not one of your students! Not me!

She pulls him up by the collar, grabs his skullcap and puts it back on his head. Afraid she'll slap him again, he shields his face with his elbows like a child.

THE MAID   Put the dagger back where it belongs, go on!

The Professor puts it in a drawer and returns.

THE MAID   Didn't I warn you just a little while ago: arithmetic leads to philology and philology leads to crime. . . .

THE PROFESSOR   You just said, "to Disaster."

THE MAID   It's the same thing.

THE PROFESSOR   Then I didn't understand you. I thought "Disaster" was a city and that you were trying to say that philology leads to the city of Disaster. . . .

THE MAID   Liar! Old fox! A scholar like you doesn't trip over the meaning of words. Don't put me on!

THE PROFESSOR (*sobbing*)   I didn't mean to kill her!

THE MAID   Are you sorry, at least?

THE PROFESSOR   Oh, yes, Marie. I swear!

THE MAID   I pity you just the same. Ah! You're a brave boy nevertheless. We'll think of something. But don't start up again. . . . It will give you a heart attack.

THE PROFESSOR   Yes, Marie. What are we going to do now?

THE MAID   Bury her . . . plus the thirty-nine others while we're at it. . . . That will come to forty coffins . . . I'll call the undertakers and my lover, Father Auguste. . . . We'll order the wreaths. . . .

THE PROFESSOR   Yes, Marie, thank you from the bottom of my heart.

THE MAID   Done. It's not worth the trouble to call Auguste, since you're a bit of a priest yourself at times, that is if one believes the gossip.

THE PROFESSOR   Now don't pick out expensive wreaths. She didn't pay for her lesson.

THE MAID   Don't worry. . . . Could you at least cover her with a tablecloth? She's indecent. Then we can carry her out.

THE PROFESSOR   Yes, Marie, yes. (*covering her*) We could get caught . . . with forty coffins. . . . You can imagine. . . . People will be amazed. And what if they want to know what's inside?

THE MAID Don't be such a worrywart. We'll say they're empty. Besides, people don't ask questions, they're used to these things.*

THE PROFESSOR Just the same . . .

The Maid takes out an armband with an insignia, perhaps a Nazi swastika.

THE MAID Hold on, if you're afraid, just put this on and you'll have nothing to fear. (*placing it around his arm*) It's just politics.

THE PROFESSOR Thank you, my little Marie, now I can breathe easy. . . . You're a good girl, Marie . . . a devoted servant. . . .

THE MAID That's enough. Let's get moving, Professor. Are you all right?

THE PROFESSOR Yes, my little Marie.

They take the young girl's corpse, one by the shoulders, the other by the legs, and head toward the door on the right.

THE PROFESSOR Be careful now. We don't want to hurt her.

They exit. The room is empty for several moments. Then the bell rings from the door on the left

THE MAID'S VOICE Just a minute! I'm coming!

She enters exactly as she did at the beginning and goes toward the door. The bell rings a second time.

---

*Author's note: In the Paris production the following two passages were dropped as well as the armband, in order not to slow down the rhythm.

THE MAID (*to herself*)   This one's certainly in a hurry! (*loud*)   Hold your horses! (*opening the door on the left.*) Good day, Mademoiselle. Are you the new student? Have you come for your lesson? The Professor is waiting for you. I'll tell him you're here. He'll be down in just a moment. Please come in, come in, Mademoiselle.

CURTAIN

Eugène Ionesco, 1909-1994, was born in Slatnia, Rumania, but lived in France for most of his life. An internationally renowned playwright and absurdist master, Ionesco profoundly altered the face of modern drama. He wrote more than twenty plays, as well as stories, memoirs and theoretical essays, and was elected a member of the French Academy.

Tina Howe's best-known plays include *Birth and After Birth, Museum, The Art of Dining, Painting Churches, Coastal Disturbances, Approaching Zanzibar,* and *Pride's Crossing,* and new translations of Eugène Ionesco's *The Bald Soprano* and *The Lesson* as well as a host of shorter plays. These works premiered at the New York Shakespeare Festival, the Kennedy Center, Second Stage, the Old Globe Theatre, Lincoln Center Theater, and the Atlantic Theater Company. Among her many awards are an Obie for Distinguished Playwriting, a Tony nomination for Best Play, an Outer Circle Critics Award, a Rockefeller Grant, two N.E.A. Fellowships, a Guggenheim Fellowship, an American Academy of Arts and Letters Award in Literature, the Sidney Kingsley Award, the New York Drama Critics' Circle Award, two honorary degrees and most recently the William Inge Award for Distinguished Achievement in the American Theatre. A two-time finalist for the Pulitzer Prize, Miss Howe has been a visiting professor at Hunter College since 1990 and has also taught master classes at NYU, UCLA, Columbia and Carnegie Mellon. Her works can be read in numerous anthologies as well as in *Coastal Disturbances: Four Plays by Tina Howe, Birth and After Birth,* and *Pride's Crossing,* published by Theatre Communications Group. Miss Howe is proud to have served on the council of the Dramatists Guild since 1990.